Making Sense of Life

A view of Christian Faith and Human Life at the beginning of the Third Millennium

Malcolm Hill

Making Sense of Life: A view of Christian Faith and Human Life at the beginning of the Third Millennium

ISBN 0 954544501

Published and produced by:
Fairway Folio
(Christian Publishing Services)
Alsager, Cheshire, UK
Tel: 01270 874662

Contents

Preface

THESE BOOKS are about life and an attempt to make sense of it. The Title has a sub-heading, including the words, 'Christian Faith'. Tragically these words may deter some readers, who may assume that the whole work may be 'blinkered' by religious dogmatism and tradition.

I hasten to deal with that assumption by affirming that the author 'takes on board' the approach of modern science: that is to say, that every attempt will be made to keep the eyes open to what is 'out there' in the 'real world'; yet realising that what is 'in there', in the unseen 'conversation' between God and human beings, and within the human mind and soul, is also real.

This open-eyed, independent stand, by the way, was the position of Jesus, whom I am called to serve as a Christian Minister. His typical words show his independent observation: *'You see this woman?'; 'Listen, a sower went out to sow'; 'Think of the ravens'*; and, *'You have heard that they were told... but what I tell you is this.'* So, I shall try to see life for myself, attempt to make sense of what I observe, and generally hope to bring a large dose of common sense and God-given intelligence to the matters of faith and conduct dealt with in this volume.

A large element in these Books is concern about 'human life'. Whilst aware that humankind is only one species among countless others on a small planet, as a human being and a Christian Minister my primary task is to 'make sense' of human life, which poses the most pressing questions and concerns for our good or ill.

Indeed the nucleus of these Books is a course used in preparing persons for Church Membership - but now expanded by means of ongoing experience, reflection and further reading in recent years. Furthermore, it is composed as an *introduction* to subjects such as study of the universe or the life and teaching of Jesus or human society, and aimed both at young people and the more mature. Also, it is the author's hope that the content may be of interest to anyone who may be investigating Church Membership and the Church's mission to human beings and human society today.

My search for truth, whether about the nature of God or the ordering of human society, is a daunting yet exciting quest. I thank God for giving me eyes to see, a mind to seek, and freedom to choose in this endeavour to MAKE SENSE OF LIFE.

Malcolm Hill, Sudbury, Suffolk, 2002

Acknowledgements

I WISH to record my thanks to those who have assisted this work in various ways. Computer production was enabled through the expertise of daughter, Lois, son-in-law, Mark, grandson, Jonathan and the wizardry of computer student, Darren Johnson. Helpful advice and encouragement came from my friend since schooldays, geologist, Dr. Geoff Gaunt, and from Rev. Colin Evans, retired URC Moderator, and Mr. Ashley Cooper, farmer-historian-author. Last but not least, Kathleen, my wife, has endured my long 'disappearances into the study', and supported me all through the five years of research and preparation.

I acknowledge also the use of computer 'software', comprising items from GSP National Curriculum Clipart, Softkey Clipart 25000, & Focus 10000 Photos Vol. 1, pictures by permission of UNA-UK from 'One World One Nation', and items from 'The Complete Encyclopaedia of Illustrations' by J.G.Heck (Gramercy).

BIBLICAL QUOTATIONS from *Revised English Bible. Copyright, Oxford University Press and Cambridge University Press.* Used by permission.

The author also wishes to acknowledge the following:

'Lord of the boundless curves of space.' Words by Albert F. Bayly (1901-84). Copyright 1988 Oxford University Press. Reproduced by permission.

'There's a spirit in the air' Words by Brian Wren (1936-) Copyright, Stainer & Bell. Used by permission.

Thanks also to the late Ray Mitchell of Long Melford, and to David Pitt of Verwood, Dorset for advice on the format and design of the original book.

A Request

The author would be grateful to receive comments or criticisms from readers. Please contact the publishers in the first instance.

MAKING SENSE OF LIFE - BOOK ONE

THE UNIVERSE, GOD & TRUTH

Part One

The Universe

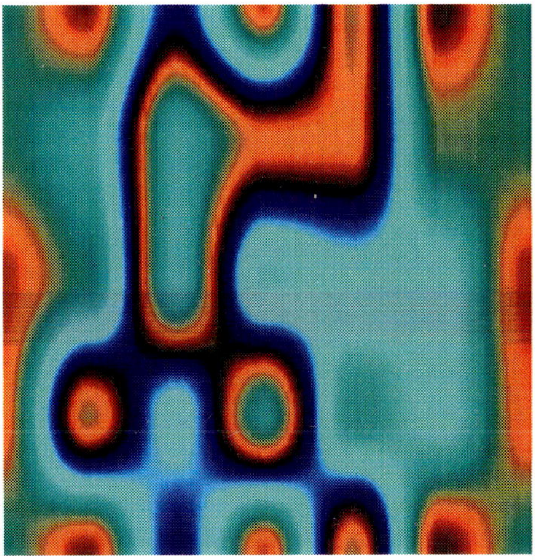

Chaos

or

Purpose?

'A Journey of a Thousand Miles Begins with the First Step.'

(Chinese Proverb)

EVEN SO, our journey into the vast universe has a pedestrian beginning. We stand at a roadside waiting to cross over. There is much traffic. If we want to cross safely, it is no good looking just one way. We must look all around, right and left.

This is an instance of a general rule: the more I observe the more I can cope with a situation. Further, the more facts I learn about life the more I am able to understand life - make sense of life.

If then we need to look around in order to cross a road, how much more do we need to survey and 'get the size' of the universe - that is, all that exists - if we are to make sense of that universe in which our life is lived. An old saying expresses our purpose just now: *'To see life steady and to see it whole.'*

NO TRIVIAL PURSUIT

THE STORY goes that a blunt Yorkshireman visited the English Lake District, an 'area of outstanding natural beauty', about which poets have penned enraptured lines. However the visitor in question, when asked to say what he thought about the mountains and lakes, replied, *'They're nowt but muck an' watter!'*

It is sadly possible to go through life with 'eyes that see not'. We can live, yet trivialise life. But our present pursuit is just the opposite: it is rather - to appreciate the stupendous universe of which we human beings are a part!

THE UNIVERSE IS BIG!!

EVERY SCHOOLCHILD knows not to look at the Sun, and certainly not through a telescope! Even at a distance of 93 million miles from us the Sun can blind us with its brilliance. It is a giant sphere, 864,000 miles in diameter, one hundred times wider than the Earth. Yet the Sun is just one of 100,000 million stars in our galaxy - and there are *many* galaxies. Moreover, recently astronomers have found the brightest known object in the universe, a quasar, that is possibly a young, distant galaxy, with a brilliancy about 100,000 billion times brighter than the Sun! So, whilst the Sun's light takes eight minutes to travel to Earth, it is estimated that the light from this quasar has been travelling for about 12 billion years! Here we have some indication of the size of the universe, and indeed of the time-span of its existence. This is where I, five feet ten inches tall, live!

THE UNIVERSE IS ENERGETIC!

ONE SUNDAY MORNING I was in the Quaker Meeting in Sudbury: an opportunity to *sit* and stare. There was a high window straight ahead through which I could see the branch of a tree against the background of sky. Suddenly the almost still-life scene was animated by a bird flying fast and horizontally past. This reminded me of another striking feature of the universe - *POWER, ENERGY.*

The immediate source of that power for us on this planet is our friend the SUN, a 'bundle of energy' if ever there was one! It has existed for billions of years, ever expending power at the rate of nine million tons of hydrogen every *second*! (Its internal temperature is 15 million degrees centigrade.)

Our EARTH is no weakling either. It is probably a spin-off from the sun, and energetically travels around it - an annual journey of 584 million miles at a speed of 66,690 mph and spins on its axis at 1000 mph. That is power! Power is also found in the movement of light, which travels at 186,000 miles per second. This gives a journey-time from London to Sydney of 1/14 of a second!

But, tracking back to where we began - the flight of a bird, we learn that a starling for example can outspeed the fastest human by flying at 30-40 mph, flapping its wings about three times every second.

Yet let's not finally demote the human being in the energy-field. Consider the human heart. It weighs only about eight ounces, but as it beats it raises 32 tons of energy each day, perhaps for a hundred years, pumping 4.5 ounces (2700 gallons) of blood every day. R.C. Macfie in *'Science Rediscovers God'* writes:

'The beating heart is a thing unique, and when we think of millions and millions of vertebrates, whales, herring, lions, crocodiles, mice and men - whose hearts never for a moment cease beating and driving the crimson fluid along, our imagination falters!'

Such is the energy of the universe!

BUT WHAT IS IT ALL ABOUT?

AS you walk along a quiet road you are faced with a big hound. The query flashes through your mind, 'Is that dog just a 'big softie', or is it part-wolf? What is the nature of the beast?' That's what you really want to know!

We are faced with a big, energetic universe. That is clear. But big and powerful as it is, we really wish to know what its nature is. That is, is it just *chaotic* -or, has it a *purpose?* Is the universe friendly, hostile - or indifferent?

Scientists in the 20th century discovered not only the size of the universe, but also evidence that it is still expanding. The result of this evidence leads some scientists to conclude that the physical universe began some 15 billion years ago. The universe according to this line of investigation was squeezed into a hot, superdense state, then in a 'big bang' it exploded, throwing its matter outwards continuously, as observed by astronomers in recent years. This view of the history and present state of the universe leads to questions of a kind asked for a long time, such as:

- *How and why did the universe begin?*
- *Is the universe unending in space and time?*
- *Does the whole process tell us of a chaos or of a purpose?*

LET US deal with these questions.

HOW AND WHY DID THE UNIVERSE BEGIN

Or perhaps, how and why did the 'big bang' happen? These questions are akin to the child's query: 'Who made God?'

However the universe came to be, whether as a 'big bang' or in some other manner as other scientists suggest, the questions, 'How?' and 'Why?' persist. We must in this instance admit that through scientific investigation we cannot at present give a satisfactory answer, because the origins of the universe are beyond the horizon of human knowledge.

When we wrestle with these 'beyond the horizon' questions, we often make the seemingly weak - but honest - comment as did my theology professor, George Phillips: *'This is a great mystery'.* And although another thoughtful man, Barry Purcell, a mining engineer, said to me: *'I don't like mysteries',* there truly are boundaries beyond which the eye cannot see and the reason cannot convince.

The queries: 'How and why did the universe come to be?' are 'beyond the horizon' queries - unless theology has an answer. (We shall consider this in *Part 2.*)

IS THE UNIVERSE UNENDING IN SPACE AND TIME?

As far as we can see there is no end to space or time. The universe *could* be endless, which would have momentous implications for us humans (as we shall see in *Book Four*). But again we cannot see beyond the horizons of space or time.

WHAT IS THE NATURE OF THE UNIVERSE?
IS IT A CHAOS OR HAS IT A PURPOSE?

We turn to an 'expert witness' in Paul Davies, the physicist. Professor Davies sums up the evidence relative to this question in his book, *'The Mind of God'*, like this:

> *'There is a class of processes, the importance of which has only recently been recognised, known as "chaotic". These are processes that exhibit no regularities. Their behaviour appears to be entirely random. It used to be thought that chaos was rather exceptional, but scientists are coming to accept that very many natural systems are chaotic, or can become so under certain circumstances. Some familiar examples are turbulent fluids, dripping taps. Even though chaos is rather common, it is clear that on the whole the universe is far from random. We recognise patterns everywhere and codify them into laws which have real predictive power. But the universe is far from being simple. It possesses a subtle kind of complexity that places it part-way between simplicity on the one hand and randomness on the other. One way of expressing this quality is to say that the universe has "organised complexity".' (p.136)*

THE UNIVERSE IS LIKE A GAME OF POOL - OR SNOOKER

PAUL DAVIES' summary of the nature of the physical universe - as a mixture of *chaos* and *purpose* - may be likened to a game of pool or snooker.

These games feature, firstly, a fixed 'frame' to the game: not only the table with raised sides and pockets, but also the specially shaped cues and variously coloured balls. These correspond to the *laws and patterns - the purposes - of nature.* Secondly, we have the human players of the game, whose skill, temperament and game-plan, in any one match are all unpredictable and variable, leading to an uncertain outcome. These correspond to the *random, uncertain elements in the activity of the universe.* Such is the universe. Such is life.

THE 'CHICKEN AND EGG' QUESTION

AS we observe the universe in operation, alongside the mixing of fixed and random aspects, we discover another duality, namely, *materials* and *ideas.*

Thus, a cook bakes a cake. The cake is a mixing of *material* ingredients such as flour, eggs and flavouring. It is also the product of an *idea* in the cook's mind. Which came first: the *material* ingredients of the cake, or the cook's *idea* of the cake?

The question can be applied to the whole *universe,* which is on the one hand a *material* colossus of galaxies in space, and on the other is a phenomenon crammed with the most complicated *ideas* - from the movements of the stars to the anatomy of a fly. So, which came first: the material of the universe, or the idea of it? The words of Edwin Conklin are apt here:

> *'The probability of life originating from accident is comparable to the probability of the unabridged dictionary resulting from an explosion in a printing shop.'*

Scientific research would not seem able to answer our question: Which came first? But again, can theology answer it? See *Part 2* of this Book!

THE THINGS THAT ARE UNSEEN AND IMMEASURABLE

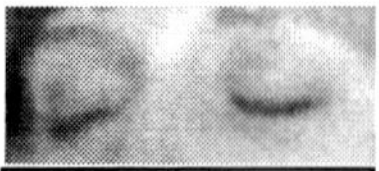

Things Unseen
thought
conscience
reason
faith
wonder
humour
hope
love

SO FAR in our view of the universe our attention has been turned chiefly toward the world 'out there'. We have noted its size and considered its workings. Yet already we have realised that the universe is not only 'out there' in space, but exists in another dimension of *ideas.* 'All that exists' includes what is '*in* there' - the thought and conscience, reason and faith, wonder and humour, hope and love. These are realities that are not seen.

Anyone then who wants to *make sense of life*, and equally wishes to live aright and happily with himself or herself, and in relationship with others - as we shall consider in *Book 3* - needs to know about and understand not only the movement of galaxies or atoms, but also the workings of the mind and the spirit - *the things that are not seen.*

A THING OF BEAUTY

WE cannot leave the question, *'What is the nature of the universe?'* without making one other observation. As we gaze at the earth's hills and valleys, seas and oceans, or the panorama of stars in space, we are aware not only of limestone rocks or green vegetation, blue water or diamond-like stellar sparkle, but also the often breathtaking beauty of the world.

So, William Wordsworth stood upon Westminster Bridge and wrote:

> *'Earth has not anything to show more fair:*

Dull would he be of soul who could pass by a sight so touching in its majesty: this city doth, like a garment, wear the beauty of the morning.'

WE may leave the city and journey north to view the magnificent beauty of Scotland, around Gruinard Bay (left).

A TRANQUIL day on the shore of Morecambe Bay (below right) gives credence to the motto of the town of Morecambe -

'BEAUTY SURROUNDS, HEALTH ABOUNDS'

THE BEAUTY of the world presses the query on our mind:

What is the nature of this magnificent universe?'

Is it just a chaotic *'tale told by an idiot... signifying nothing'*?

Or is it part of *'one enormous plan'*?

Has a Personal, beauty-loving GOD conceived it all?

Has God invited us to take an endless journey together, beginning on Earth?

Read on!

MAKING SENSE OF LIFE - BOOK ONE

THE UNIVERSE, GOD AND TRUTH

Part Two

The Personal God

Personality

Artistry

Queen honey bee - tended by her workers

Attention to detail

Generosity

CAN WE believe in a PERSONAL GOD?

Daily Gossip

VICAR DOESN'T BELIEVE IN GOD

THE ANSWER we shall give is: 'YES!' - To which the response from many a Churchgoer would be: 'I should think so! What's a 'Reverend' doing , if he doesn't so believe? When he prays is he merely musing?' Yet, more than once in recent years headlines have screamed from tabloid newspapers.

Though it may seem a foregone conclusion that a cleric - or indeed any member of the Christian Church - should believe in a Personal God, the matter is not clear-cut. When asked, 'What do you mean by God?', answers may vary from a very much human-like, 'anthropomorphic' Being - the Old Man in the Sky with the stern look, pictured in one's childhood (right)- to a vague 'Power' akin to the *'elan vital'*, 'thrusting force' behind evolution, proposed by the philosopher, Bergson.

THE CASE AGAINST A PERSONAL GOD

ANY believer in a Personal God is clearly faced by formidable arguments against. It seems preposterous to some to believe that this vast physical universe is the product of a Person. Is it not presumptuous for us puny human beings to deem our place in the universe to be so important, and then proceed to fashion God in our image? Can we justify belief in a Personal God?

HUMILITY AND WONDER BEFORE GOD

WE may see the force of the argument *against* a Personal God, yet make out a case *for.* Firstly we may point out that it is not with any feeling of self-importance that we believe that God is Personal. Well over two millennia ago the sense of humble wonder was expressed by the Hebrew Psalmist:

> *'When I look up at your heavens, the work of your fingers'*
> *at the moon and the stars you have set in place,*
> *what is a frail mortal, that you should be mindful of him,*
> *a human being, that you should take notice of him!' (Psalm 8.3,4)*

The same attitude is found in the words of King Solomon as he dedicated his Temple in Jerusalem to the worship of God:

> *'But can God indeed dwell on earth?*
> *Heaven itself, the highest heaven cannot*
> *contain you;how much less this house that I*
> *have built!' (1 Kings 8.27)*

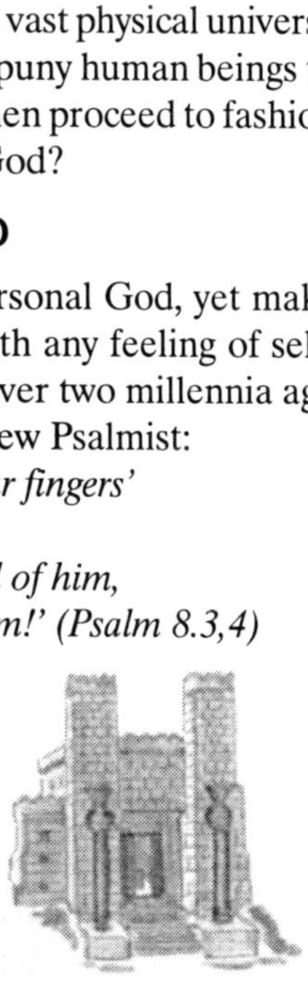

Hebrew prophets also are wary of fashioning God in human dimension. So we read these words in the Book of Isaiah:

> *'What likeness then will you find for God... an image which a craftsman makes..?*
> *To whom then will you liken me, whom set up as my equal? asks the Holy One*
> *Lift up your eyes to the heavens: consider who created these (stars)... ' (40.18,19,25,26)*

Yet, often 'God' is crafted in human image (right).

Athena Promachos (Defender of the City) is shown in the menacing pose of a human warrior. Thor, the Germanic god, is envisaged holding his own threatening hammer.

Contrast the insight of the prophet, Hosea *(11.9)* - God speaks:

> *'I am not going to let loose my fury... for I am God, not a mortal;... I shall not come with threats.'*

Many believers, then, are aware of the pitfalls in arguing the case for a Personal God, yet respond with reasons why they should persevere in the quest.

THE CASE FOR A PERSONAL GOD

IT IS IMPORTANT to clarify two issues as we begin to make our case in favour.

REALITIES OF SCIENCE AND BEYOND

THE FIRST ISSUE concerns the relation of science to belief in God. *Science*, as commonly understood, studies the material world, the 'things that are seen'. Some people have denied the existence of an unseen, spiritual world, and include in this denial the existence of a Personal God. Such a view is sometimes called *'naturalism'*. Theologian, Langdon Gilkey, writing in *'Science and Religion'*, notes the consequences of naturalism's view: *'The naturalistic world-view is an extension of scientific understanding beyond the range of science.'* Thus, we cannot assert a drop of water as a 'fact', and then deny a pang of conscience as a 'fact'. Both are real. So, the unseen Personal God may well be a reality alongside and related to the seen universe, just as a human being's spirit exists alongside and related to the physical body.

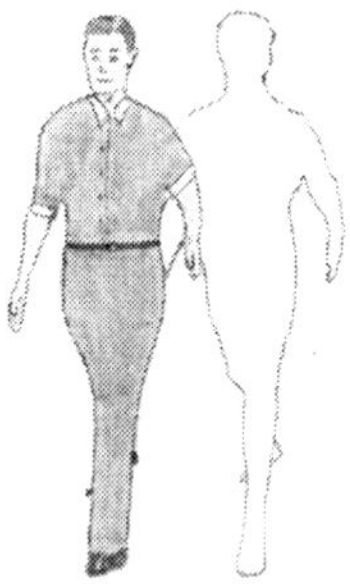

WHAT DO WE MEAN BY THE *'PERSONAL GOD'?*

THE SECOND ISSUE concerns the meaning of *'God'* - to begin with. The meaning was finely stated by the Theologian, Archbishop Anselm: *'GOD is a being than which a greater cannot be conceived.'* Or, to put it in negative form: God would not be God for us, if the Deity were found to be less than some other being. This definition of 'God' has an acute bearing on the question: *'Which came first, the physical universe or the idea of the universe?'* The definition implies that God comes first - as the greatest Being, rising above (transcending) both the physical universe and the idea that fashioned (created) the universe. God, according to the definition is both the author or creator of all space and time *and* the originator of all ideas that 'shaped' space and time.

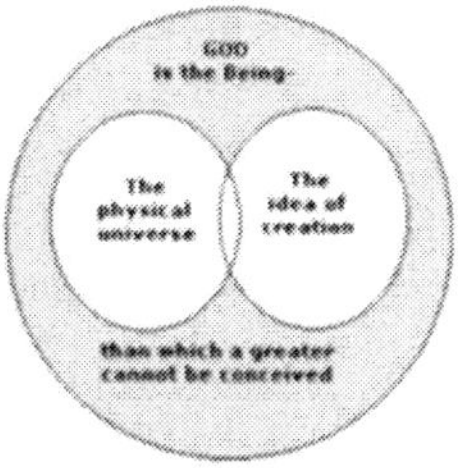

The definition however does not constitute a proof that God exists, but is most valuable as an accurate description of the supreme meaning of 'God' for the belie- ver. It provides a fully adequate frame for a reasonable and comprehensive religious faith. So, we can now proceed to describe the *'Personal God'* -

'PERSONAL' Who is a 'person'? A 'person' is a living being with an amalgam of qualities, principally:

self consciousness	ability to communicate
intelligence	a sense of beauty and joy
inventiveness	care for the self and others

'PERSONAL GOD'

WE now put 'personal' and 'God' together. Thus, by PERSONAL GOD we mean:

> *GOD, the Being transcending all that exists, material and spiritual,is a PERSON with self-consciousness, intelligence, inventiveness, ability to communicate, a sense of beauty and joy,and care for the self and others.*

We can now expand on this summary definition.

GOD THE CREATOR

THE theologian, Nikolai Berdyaev, says that creativeness:

> *'... is always a growth, an addition, the making of something that has not existed in the world before... a bringing forth out of nothing'.*

Such an act of creation is suggested in the first words of the Bible:

> *'In the beginning God created the heavens and the earth.'*

God however is not only to be thought of as making a unique creation 'in the beginning', but as continuously creating as Paul Davies contends in *'The*

Mind of God':

'Many people have an image of God as a sort of pyrotechnic engineer, lighting a blue touch-paper to ignite the Big bang, and then sitting back to watch the show.'

Davies goes on to quote the physicist, Russell Stannard:

'Just as an author does not write the first chapter, and leave the others to write themselves, so God's creativity is not to seem as uniquely confined to... the event of the Big Bang. Rather his creativity is to be seen as permeating equally all space and time: his role as creator and Sustainer merge.' (p.58)

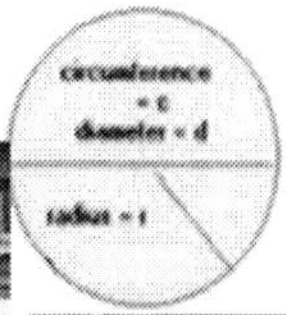

We may understand God's continual creation as we observe our human race's continual creative acts, for example:

scientific theories

artistic compositions

the formation of new human relationships in marriage.

This concept of God's continual creation is captured well in a hymn by A. F. Bayly:

'Lord of the boundless curves of space and time's deep mystery,
to your creative might we trace all nature's energy.
Your mind conceived the galaxy, each atom's secret planned
and every age of history your purpose. Lord, has spanned.'

GOD THE DESIGNER-ARTIST

IT is debatable whether the motor car is a perfect blessing to humankind! But such a doubt will not cross the mind of a young man just having acquired his first automobile. It will be his 'pride and joy'! He will lift up the bonnet to reveal the spanking-new engine, and examine its detailed designs with awe and wonder: the gearbox, carburettor, alternator, oil-filter, hoses, spark-plugs, battery - to name only some of the interactive parts of the total design, and each of which has unique design details.

Just so, our awe and wonder of the natural world is in the details of its design - and artistry.

We note, for example, the situation of the Earth, firstly in its relation to the Sun. The distance between is such that it is neither too hot nor too cold for life to flourish. Its axis is tilted at such an angle as it orbits the Sun as to provide

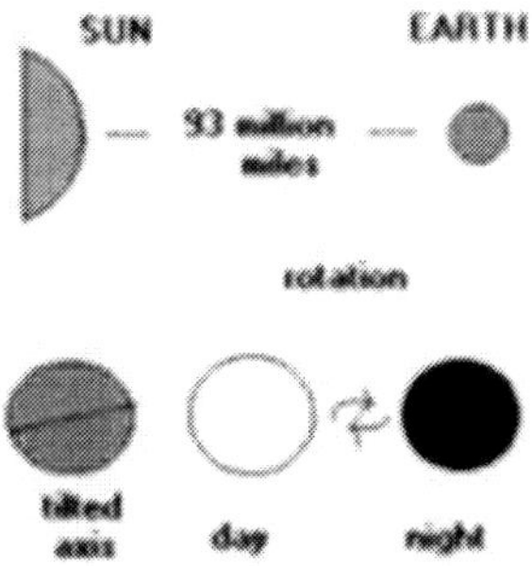

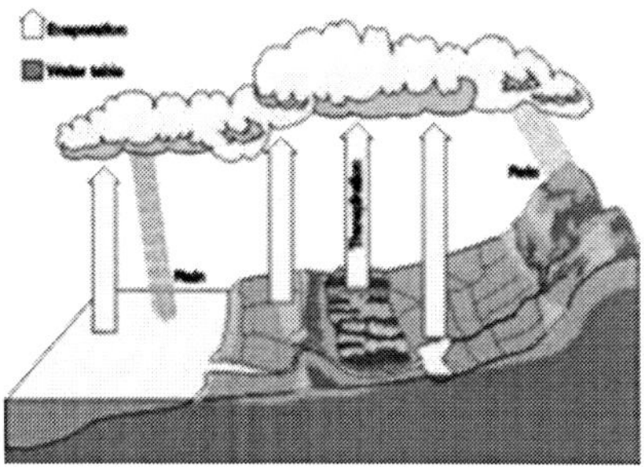

the four seasons with their varied air-pressures, winds and rain-clouds, vital to the growth of myriads of living beings on land, sea and air. It also rotates to give the contrasts of day and night. The spinning of the Earth and the varying temperatures of the seasons cause air pressures to be high then low, leading to wind, cloud formation & rain.

THE WONDER OF THE SEASONS

WINTER

Season of nature's rest... yet all creatures are called upon to harden and endure

SPRING

A time of revival, new growth, restored loveliness and exertion.
A season of hope.

SUMMER

The crowning glory of the year.
Time to garner the planet's bounty.
A season for vacation... for basking in the creation

AUTUMN

Season of faded glory? Hardly... with its continuing fruitfulness and splashes of a myriad brilliant colours.

THROUGH all the seasons the rivers flow - as the 'arteries' of the 'body' of the land.

AS the axis of the Earth is slightly tilted, its journey around the Sun means that, now its northern hemisphere is closer to the Sun's radiation and then its southern hemisphere. This gives us a warm season and a cold one with two in between, when both hemispheres receive equal radiation.

The Sun - and Earth with its seasons - are gigantic instances of design compared to the microscopic *cellular bacterium.* Such life-cells are measured in *microns*, that is, millionths of a metre. Yet each bacterium contains proteins, nucleic acids, fats and carbohydrates necessary for life, and organised in a complex way. Design, ingenuity, intelligence permeate the universe - in the whole, and in the minutest parts.

Yet in nature we not only find amazing design, but also exquisite beauty. Again, it is seen both in the large, as an astronaut views the colourful Earth from space - and in the small, as we gaze through a microscope at a hexagonal snow flake. Each snowflake has its own pretty design within the hexagon!

Christian theology sees God as the Designer-Artist of the detail of the universe. There is no proof of this scientifically. Yet by no stretch of the imagination could we call it absurd to believe that this is so. Believers have for long had the faith that the design and artistry observed in the world of nature are the work of the intelligent God with a love of beauty.

> *'God only is the Maker of all things near and far;*
> *He paints the wayside flower; He lights the evening star.'*
> *(Matthias Claudius)*

GOD – THE COMMUNICATOR

WE included in our list of the abilities of the Personal God, *'communicator'*. This is a key Divine ability. It would indeed be very odd if God, the greatest Being, had made creatures such as humans who desire and are able to communicate thoughts and wishes, but was unable - or unwilling- to communicate Himself. God would then be inferior to his creatures: articulate man; inarticulate God!

An important aspect of God's communication with humankind is *understanding.* Paul Davies, on the last page of his book, *'The Mind of God'*, describes this, as follows:

> *'The central theme that I have explored in this book is that, through science, we human beings are able to grasp some at least of nature's secrets... Why this should be, just why Homo Sapiens should carry the spark of rationality that provides the key to the universe, is a deep enigma.'*

A vivid instance of God's 'speaking' to the human understanding was given by the author of Psalm 19 (vv.1-4) :

> *'The heavens tell out the glory of God,*
> *heaven's vault makes known his handiwork.*
> *One day speaks to another, night to night imparts knowledge,*
> *and this without speech or language or sound of any voice.*
> *Their sign shines forth on all the earth,*
> *their message to the ends of the world.'*

The stars in the vastness of space 'speak' of the immense concept in God's mind; of the steadfastness of God's purpose; not to mention the brightness and joy in the 'heart' of God.

As a man or woman reveals good character through an attempt to rescue a swimmer in trouble, so God reveals his character through his works of creation, and the sustenance of nature. God 'sings a song without words', but full of meaning and delight.

We shall add more detail about God's messages in our next section, and in *Part 3.*

THE PERSONAL GOD WHO LOVES US

THE most essential trait of God is love. *'Love'* itself needs explanation. What is *'love'? Love* is both an inner attitude and a relationship between persons. *Love* is also a mixture of *affection* and *respect. Affection* is a strong feeling of delight and goodwill toward another person. *Respect* acts through our conscience: we are aware of right and wrong treatment of another person, and when we respect we choose to do the right.

Such *love* - respect and affection - is the most valuable experience we can enjoy. It meets our deepest need - the need of our *soul (or 'spirit').*

Here we must consider the human *SOUL*, because it is itself the most worthy entity that exists. It is the *soul* that God loves.

What is the 'soul'? *(See also Book 3, Part 1, pp. 72-75)*

THE SOUL IS UNIQUE

The perceptive observer will see that no two human faces are exactly alike. Each is *unique!* The same is true of each human soul. I am like no one else. I do not share my soul with anyone else.

THE SOUL IS CREATED

MY soul - like a piece of furniture - did not make itself!
It was created by God through God's bounty and love.

THE SOUL IS GROWING

LIKE most of creation - certainly plants and animals - my soul grows moment by moment by means of all its emotions and thoughts, and its relations with other people and events. So, my soul develops in awareness and mastery continuously.

THE SOUL IS FREE

MY soul is a 'free agent' by God's design. Through the decision and conscience I can choose to walk or sit down, to do right or wrong, to love or hate - and so learn the 'lessons' of living, now and always.

THE SOUL IS A VESSEL

MY soul is like a *vessel* such as a jug. It is made to be filled with something valuable, be it water or wine. The soul is meant to be filled with the love of God its Maker and with the love of other souls.

THE SOUL IS LOVED BY GOD

GOD loves every human soul. God has respect and affection for my soul, and , as the 'Greatest Being', possesses love to the highest degree. This is how a Hebrew poet expressed it over 2000 years ago:

> *'As the heavens tower high above the earth,*
> *so outstanding is God's love towards those*
> *who respect him.' (Psalm 103.11)*

So, human souls have experienced the *outstanding* love of God over several millennia.

Jesus' experience of God was unmistakably personal and loving. He addressed God as *'Abba', 'Father',* and taught about God's caring love in this simile:

> *'Would any of you offer his son a stone when he asks for bread, or a snake when he asks for a fish? If you, bad as you are, know how to give good things to your children, how much more will your heavenly Father give good things to those who ask him?' (Matthew 7.9-11)*

An early Christian, John, reflecting on the life and teaching of Jesus, wrote:

'God is love. This is how he showed his love among us. he sent his only Son into the world that we might have life through him. This is what love really is: not that we have loved God, but that he loved us..' (1st Letter of John 4.8-10)

Elizabeth Fry

Now we take just one example from the centuries of history since Biblical times. Elizabeth Fry, the Quaker, who visited the awful London prisons to care for and reform convicted people, tells of the growth of her reception of God's love:

> *'My heart began to feel itself silenced before God..*
> *I felt myself under the shadow of the wing of God...*
> *and as I walked home by starlight,*
> *I looked through nature up to nature's God.'*

Further, in a prayer, she called on the resources of God's love:

> *'Enable me, O Lord, to feel tenderly and charitably to all my fellow mortals... Let me walk in all humility and godly fear before all men, and in Thy sight. Amen.'*

May this author quote two of his own experiences - in line with the dedication in the Preface - 'to see life for myself'.

GOD'S LOVE IN AN ATTIC

THE teenage period of life is for many a time of searching for the basic truths of life, including the longing for loving relationships. If at that time a young person loses a parent by death, as I did aged 14, the search becomes more pressing. I could now take the reader to the attic in my hometown where I had the overwhelming feeling of being loved by God. Was this feeling a substitute for the loss of my father? Not entirely, I believe. My recollection is that I was receiving love from my Maker; a wider love than my human father could have provided. My whole life was being loved by God. A verse from John Bowring's hymn fits my experience:

'GOD is love: his mercy brightens all the path in which we rove;
Bliss he wakes and woe he lightens; God is wisdom, God is love.'

My whole life 'being loved by God' is further explained by the second experience.

GOD'S LOVE ON A MOUNTAIN

I and three of my friends all aged about 19 undertook a Youth Hostel tour to the English Lake District at Easter time. We intended one day to walk from Wasdale to Eskdale over the Sca Fell range by way of the high pass called Mickledore (arrowed on the sketch). We were full of high spirits, but bereft of anything that could be called 'mountaineering equipment'! We began the trek up the mountain in bright morning sunshine, but soon snow was falling heavily. This made the climb for us more exciting, especially when we slid a couple of times down the steep scree. Soon however we were cutting every step out of the deepening snow, and high spirits changed into an ominous sense of danger. We discussed what we should do. Turning back down the mountain to walk an extra five miles by an easier route did not at first appeal, not least to our pride. Yet the alternative could be to sustain serious injury - or worse. Discussion among us mirrored that within me. The choice between good sense and pride, between the will to live and throwing life away, became acute. The 'reserves' of my belief that God had given me my life through his love, and wanted me to live, were summoned, and I decided that I should make every effort to choose good sense and survive. 'I'm turning back', I said to my friends. We all retreated from the mountain, and looking back at its foot we saw how near to becoming 'climbing fatalities' we had been! Reflecting later still, I realised that my life had been loved and saved by God, and this is my own evidence for the love of the Personal God.

END THOUGHT from ANDREW HARVEY

> *'The glory Jesus saw and knew in God was a glory not merely of omnipotent power and knowledge, but, above and beyond that, a glory of love, a love so boundless, so overflowing, and so continually self-outpouring in every way... The parable that most clearly reveals the originality and daring of Jesus' vision of the love of God is that of the Prodigal Son.' ('Son of Man', p.8)*

THE GENEROUS GOD

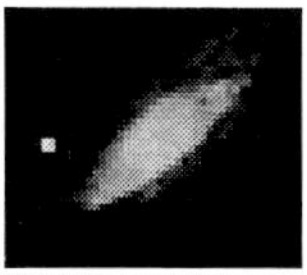

WHEN we look into the sky what do we see? During the day we may look out, beyond the clouds, into an endless azure vault. At night, we may view the stars and galaxies. By day or night we are impressed by the size of the universe. The remotest object we could see with our naked eye in the night sky, the Great Galaxy in Andromeda, is 13,000,000,000,000,000,000 miles distant from us! What word can describe that? We turn to the thesaurus for suggestions: *immense, unbounded, vast, gigantic, infinite!* But what does the size of the universe tell us about its Creator?

Firstly, it speaks of what God is *not*: small-minded, petty, grudging, stingy, mean, cheese-paring, parsimonious. On the contrary, the universe 'speaks volumes' about God's bounty, open-handedness, munificence, liberality and *generosity.*

Even this planet, tiny by comparison, proclaims God's generosity. The Psalmist (65.12,13) looked on Palestine over 2000 years ago and told of God's bounty:

> *'You crown the year with your good gifts;*
> *places where you have passed drip with plenty;*
> *... the meadows are clothed with sheep*
> *and the valleys decked with grain.'*

Two millennia later Earth's pastures and hills remain fertile! Can you recall the last time you went to your local market and found the vegetable or bread stalls empty?'

Over 2000 years separate the Hebrew psalmist and the Victorian hymn-writer, George Rawson, but both appreciate God's generosity:

> *'You produce grain from the earth,*
> *food to sustain the people's strength,*
> *and wine to gladden their hearts... ' (Psalm 104.15)*

'The old thankful story shall scale Thine abode,
Thou King of all glory, most bountiful God.'
(From the Hymn, 'With gladness we worship.')

THE PATIENT GOD

'ROME wasn't built in a day.' 600 years BC. the city was developing from a collection of mud-hut villages. Then the Forum, the open market place, was built, soon to be lined with two rows of shops. Year by year construction continued: so the Capitol was built in 506 BC.; the Temple of Apollo in 431; the Aqua Appia aqueduct in 312; the Tabularium in 73; the Colosseum in 80 AD. Century by century Rome grew through the time of the Republic, then the Empire before Christ, and into the Christian era. Truly, 'Rome was *not* built in a day.'! - This saying, as *'Brewer's Dictionary of Phrase and Fable'* well puts it, means that *'worthwhile tasks are not accomp-lished without patient persev-erance and a considerable interval of time'*

Yet the centuries of Rome's building are but a 'twinkling of an eye' compared with the time of the development of God's universe - a span perhaps of 15 billion years! One stage of that evolution perseveringly followed an-other.

God's *'worthwhile task'* of building the world shows God's *'patient perse-verance'*.

The Patience of God

The Universe develops - in billions of years

15	12	10	6	4	2	TODAY
			Solar system formed	Earth formed		

Life on Earth develops

3.5	2	1	TODAY
Microscopic life	Green algae	Trilobytes (ancestors of insects & lobsters	

The last 500 million years

500	400	300	200	100	TODAY
Molluscs	Fish	Reptiles	Birds	Mammals	
Mosses		Insects		Humans	

We shall expand the significance of God's patience when we consider the struggle between good and evil in *Book Three, Part 1,* and also the prospects for humankind's future in *Book Four, Part 2.* For now let another Hebrew Psalmist capture the wonder of God's time and patience:

> *'In your sight a thousand years are as the passing of one day or as a watch in the night.'(Psalm 90.4)*

TINY IS PRECIOUS TO GOD

ONE of the most amazing features of the universe is that side-by-side with immensity is the miniature. Vast deserts are the sum of tiny grains of sand! One of the smallest items of matter is the sub-atomic particle: ten billions of them stretched out in a row might measure one centimetre! I——I

When we turn to organic beings we may exemplify the smallest known insect, the hairy-winged beetle which measures 2/10 of a millimetre. Consider also that these tiny creatures produce minute eggs! The eggs too of a parasitic wasp are so small and light that there would be 141,750,000 of them to an ounce!

The contrast between the gigantic and the microscopic in the cosmos tells us something important about God. The greatness of God consists in this combination of the immense plan and the minute care for detail with concern for each individual creature. The Psalmist notes God's personal care for him, one small human being (Psalm 139.1,5)

> *'Lord, you have examined me and know me.*
> *You know all, whether I sit down or rise up..*
> *You have kept close guard before me and behind,*
> *and have spread your hand over me.'*

Jesus pursues the theme:

> *'Fear not, even the hairs of your head have all been counted... not one sparrow can alight upon the ground without God's knowledge.'(Matthew 10.29-30)*

In this immense universe tiny is precious to God.

GOD'S WONDERFUL MASTER GAME PLAN

WE likened the universe to a 'game of pool or snooker'. As in any game, God has so arranged the cosmos to include both *laws* and *randomness, patterns* and *uncertainty.* Both of these features are vital for God's purposes.

The existence of laws and randomness *together* fashions a world with a very advantageous combination: patterns supply the element of *reliability* (laws of nature), enabling living beings to gain confidence and plan ahead; and uncertainty supplies the element of *freedom, adventure and hope.* This paradox or partnership of opposites is wonderful; it is GOD'S MASTER GAME-PLAN! - for what?

IS not this the PURPOSE of the PLAN?

To produce, through the universe of matter and ideas, living beings,
who at one and the same time, can learn from God and their
experience both to be responsible, law-abiding and reliable,
and to have freedom of choice, independence of thought,
and the ability to accept love and show love.

The poet, John Keats, seems to agree with this plan for life in the world: it is *'the vale of soul-making'*.

Being assured of this 'master-plan', we can proceed far in *making sense* of the sometimes tragic, topsy-turvy circumstances we undergo in our journey of life.

(We shall consider this in more detail in *Book Three, Part 1.)*

WHO is the PERSONAL GOD?

GOD is the Supreme Being;
the Person whose intelligent Mind, Soul of beauty,
and love of other beings
created - and continues to create - the universe.
God builds it with generosity, patience and attention to detail,
and care for each and every creature.
God has so arranged all that exists
as to produce beings who can share
God's ideas, creativity, responsibility and, above all,
LOVE.

MAKING SENSE OF LIFE - BOOK ONE

THE UNIVERSE, GOD AND TRUTH

Part Three

How Do You Know?

Free-thinking, Bible-believing, or...

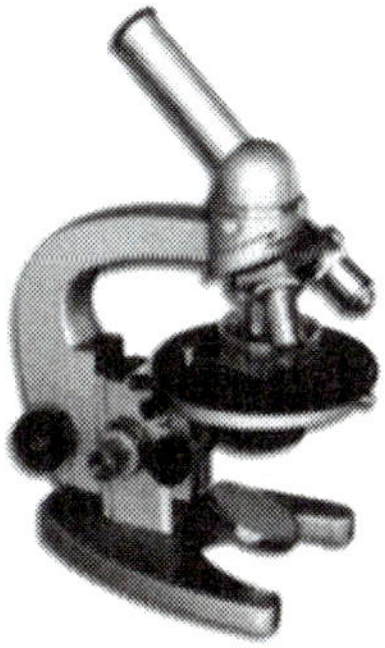

observation, reason, revelation...

discernment of Scripture...

AN 'INTERRUPTION'

PART THREE of this Book is an 'interruption'.

The author is in 'full flight' in his theme, when a listener butts in politely, to say: "Hang on: before you go any further in trying to explain life, God, the universe and everything else, I'd like you to tell me how you know that what you are saying is true. How *do* you know? With what authority do you write?"

OBSERVATION, REASON & REVELATION

LET US begin an answer with a comparison. Suppose we are travelling by car in an unfamiliar region. We approach a town, but the place-name sign is missing! How do we know which town it is? - Shortly we see a hospital with its signboard proclaiming *OLDCASTLE GENERAL HOSPITAL.* Soon, on the opposite side of the road there is a football stadium with *OLDCASTLE ROVERS F.C.* blazoned on its main stand. We stop at traffic-lights; there is a hotel and at its entrance a sign, reading, *OLDCASTLE ROTARY CLUB MEETS HERE.* We reach our destination, the Town Hall, to meet an old friend who is now the Mayor of Oldcastle. He greets us in his parlour. Now we are in no doubt in which town we are!

How do we know? -

- By several pieces of observation: the signs, each agreeing with the others.
- By reason, which connects and makes sense of the observations.
- Through revelation - the Mayor of Oldcastle reveals that we are actually in the place where we intended to be, Oldcastle Town Hall!

Observation, reason and revelation give us *knowledge...* and not just of material things, but also of moral and spiritual experiences.

Let us take as an example God's Providence. We stand on high ground and scan the country around. We may see a patchwork of fields with varied crops, or with their flocks of sheep.

What does our *observation* tell us? 'Here is abundant provision!' Then our *reason* tells us about the 'mechanism' of the country-side: the Sun, fertile soil, rain, insects, worms and more that generates the abundance.

Then we have the *revelation* by the Creator-God, who provides the 'mechanism', telling us of God's love for all creatures.

A vital element in this basis of knowledge is *human* observation and reason. However, there are many religious believers who would frown on reliance upon such 'free-thought' in deciding moral and spiritual matters. Is their objection valid?

THE AUTHORITY OF 'HOLY SCRIPTURE'

THIS POSTER (right) appeared on a chapel wall in the Rhondda:

> 'TRUST IN THE LORD WITH ALL THINE HEART, AND LEAN NOT UNTO THINE OWN UNDERSTANDINGS'
> *Proverbs 3.5*

May we not find here at least a hint that religious faith is being opposed to human understanding? Such opposition in truth has prevailed in many societies where religious writings have been treated as *HOLY SCRIPTURE* or *GOD'S WORD.*

How did this happen?

God communicates/reveals himself -his morality and affection- always to anyone who 'listens', and sometimes God's messages are recorded in writing by human scribes. The Biblical scholar, Georg Fohrer, in his *'Introduction to the Old Testament'* maps out the varied origins of that 'book of books', as 'Holy Scripture', like this:

- the notion that the written word has magical powers (Numbers 5.11)
- religious and moral teaching of the Israelite prophets is accepted as God's message (Amos 2.6-16)
- accounts of the occupation of Canaan by the patriarchs provide a religious and legal claim to the land (Genesis 35.11,12)
- codes of law regulating life and conduct are based upon God's will (Leviticus 27.34).

These varied strands were woven together into the Jewish 'Holy Scripture' in the centuries immediately before Christ, so that the historian, Josephus, in 100 AD., refers to a collection of 22 Books, consisting of the Pentateuch (Or Five Books of Moses); 13 Books of Prophecy; and 4 Books of Hymns and Precepts. These are to be sacred, and their text not to be tampered with: they are 'Holy Scripture'.

The early Christians, many of them Jews, therefore regarded the Jewish Scriptures as 'Holy'. Thus, we discover in the Christian Gospels the phrase, *'scripture says'*. New Testament authors believe the Israelite prophets to have been divinely inspired, and their predictions to have come to fruition in the life of Jesus. The next step, then, was to regard their own writing about Jesus as God's 'Messiah' and 'Word' as sacred. Indeed Origen, the 3rd century theologian, affirmed:

> *'The sacred books were not the works of human beings; they were*

written by the inspiration of the Holy Spirit at the will of the Father of all through Jesus Christ.' (De Principiis 4.9)

This belief in the divine inspiration of the 'Bible', as the combined Jewish and Christian Scriptures are generally known, and their supreme authority for Christians and the Church, has been established in much the greater part of Christendom from the time of Origen. It continued through the medieval and Reformation periods, and is widespread still in the 21st century. Three quotations will endorse this situation.

'The authority of the Holy Scripture... dependeth not on the testimony of any man or church; but wholly upon God (who is truth itself) the author thereof... Our full persuasion and assurance of the infallible truth and divine authority thereof is from the inward work of the Holy Spirit, bearing witness by and with the Word in our hearts... Nothing is at any time to be added - whether by new revelations of the Spirit or by the traditions of men... The church is finally to appeal to them.' (Westminster Confession of Faith, Presbyterian, 1643)

The Book of
Common Prayer,
The Church of England;
Psalter or Psalms of David,

'Holy Scripture containeth all things necessary to salvation: so that whatsoever is not read therein, nor may be proved thereby, is not to be required of any man, that it should be believed as an Article of the Faith, or to be thought requisite or necessary to salvation.' (Book of Common Prayer, Articles of Religion, VI, Church of England, 1662)

These two quotations came out of the 'stable' of the Protestant Reformation, and regard Holy Scripture very much as the bulwark against what they deemed to be the errors of the (Roman) Catholic 'unscriptural' practices, such as the Mass.

However the Catholic Church also upholds the sacredness of the Bible; the First Vatican Council (1870) affirmed that the Scriptures *'have God as their Author'.*

FREE-THINKING OR BIBLE-BELIEVING... A DILEMMA

THE CHRISTIAN CHURCH, by and large, whether Catholic or Reformed - or Orthodox or Pentecostal - affirms the supreme authority of the Bible as the 'Word of God'. Its text should not be altered, and its words are true, that is, without fault or error factually, morally and spiritually. This belief puts anyone

Observation *Reason* *Experience* *Divine Revelation*	*versus*	*Infallible Bible* *Church Authority*

in a dilemma, who either through observation, reason or experience concludes that a passage in the Bible *is* in error, whether in fact or in moral or spiritual truth.

Here there have arisen two competing authorities.

This is an acute problem for some faithful Christians, including this author. Let us see it in a parable:

> *Suppose you have a good friend, one for whom you have both affection and respect because of his or her general wisdom and behaviour. But further suppose that this friend either says something that is factually untrue or behaves on one occasion in a way that is wrong. You would not be human in that event, if you didn't, just for a moment, hesitate to criticise your respected friend.*

The Bible - The Word of God?

The case is similar for someone who is trying to make sense of life and seeking the truth. (And what is *truth?* - Basically *truth* is *'words and statements that agree with material facts or spiritual experiences'*.)

So, when a person has been nurtured in a religious tradition, and taught to regard the Bible as 'the word of God', he or she may experience the dilemma in this form. He or she will love and respect their tradition and scriptures, because of their positive support and the wise guidance. Hence there could be hesitation, if there arises any cause for criticism or questioning of the truth of that tradition. That is exactly the dilemma of this author.

TRUTH AND GOOD ADVICE IN THE BIBLE

THIS AUTHOR has been nurtured in the Christian tradition all his conscious life. Sefton Road Congregational Church, Morecambe provided his spiritual and cultural home, family and friends from the age of three. The largest ingredient in his spiritual and mental diet has been the Bible, whether 'served up' in Church worship, group and private study, or in theological college and

university. His resulting regard for the Bible and other Christian literature has been more than that of a 'good read'. So much in the Bible has been an inspiration. For example:

> *'Bless the Lord, O my soul; and all that is within me,*
> *bless his holy name!*
> *... forget none of his benefits, who forgives all your iniquity,*
> *who heals all your diseases..' (Psalm 103.1-3)*

These words of the Psalmist tell of my deep thanksgiving for life's bounties.

Other Biblical passages have given courage to face up to the challenges of life: once, anticipating deep hostility at a meeting, fear was overridden by the words of Psalm 23, verse 4:

> *'Though I walk through a valley dark as death, I will fear no evil;*
> *God's rod and staff they comfort me.'*

Unfair people may have had their 'knives out' for you, but God is 'wielding his club', a real match for your adversaries! The author coped with his ordeal.

Here is an example of good advice from the Bible:

> *'Why do you see the speck in your brother's eye, and fail to see the plank in your own? First take the plank from your eye, then you will see clearly to take the speck out of your brother's. (Matthew 7.3,4)*

This is a timely warning against hasty criticism and an encouragement to self-examination that can save us from moral blindness.

So, the Bible earns deep respect and affection, such as is indicated in the commendation of the Book of Books at the coronation of a British monarch.

> *'We present you with this Book, the most*
> *valuable thing this world affords. Here*
> *is wisdom; this is the royal Law; these*
> *are the lively Oracles of God.'*

Anyone then, who has found Divine inspiration, moral encouragement and tried and tested advice from words in the Bible will not find it easy to admit it, should he find errors therein, or otherwise be critical of its contents.

THE NUB OF THE PROBLEM, A 'HOLY SCRIPTURE' TOO FAR

WE have given examples of truth and good advice found in the Bible. We shall soon proceed to cite what in all honesty we see as contradictions, wrong advice and unworthy theology in the Bible. (We must not be less honest in assessing words in the Bible than we would be elsewhere.)

But how, the whole Bible-believing Christian will ask in horror, do you propose to explain how errors appear in the Bible?

This is the nub of the problem, and the explanation is *the failure of those who compiled the Bible to discriminate between the passages of genuine inspiration, and those of lesser quality.* The compilers put all in - good and bad.

The Bible critic hastens to add that it is not his purpose to debunk the Bible, but to try sincerely to understand its contents, and to sift out its most important truths. His aim also is to warn the seeker against indiscrimination, because the fact is that a *core* of divinely-inspired writing has had attached to it other literature of lesser worth. Here we may compare 'Holy Scripture' with 'Holy Church'. Geoffrey Chaucer in *'Canterbury Tales'* noted the difference between two churchmen: whereas the sincere, poor parson *'taught Christ's law...*

and first followed it himself", the pardoner *'feigned flattery and japes (tricks)... and made the person and the people his apes (dupes)'.* It is no different with 'Holy Scripture'. At certain points Jewish and Christian compilers and authorities have extended 'holiness' from the core of the Bible to its surrounding errors with insufficient discrimination. The result is a *scripture too far!* The nub of a big problem!

The enormity and tragedy of this problem is that the critic/seeker-after-truth is believed to be affronting God and God's 'Word', and is often threatened with dire consequences, or deemed to be 'in league with the Devil'!

THE RIGHT TO CRITICISE THE BIBLE

THE Bible-critic protests that he loves God too much to affront God. He is trying to be honest and realistic about the Bible. If he finds inconsistency, or wrong advice or theology, he must acknowledge it. As we proceed to learn of how the Biblical personalia and authors developed in knowledge and faith, and as we come across the errors and less worthy passages, we shall realise why we have the right and indeed the duty to our fellowmen to criticise the Bible

HOW DID THE KNOWLEDGE AND FAITH OF THE BIBLICAL AUTHORS DEVELOP?

'My knowledge is partial', wrote Paul *(1 Corinthians 13.12)* *'We only have earthenware jars to hold this treasure (the gospel of God)', (2 Corinthians 4.7),* Paul again admitted. Such admissions of imperfection by a Biblical author are genuine, and clearly to be expected by anyone who understands human nature. Most of our knowledge and faith is accumulated step-by-step: we stumble and toddle as we learn to walk.

The one who achieves copperplate handwriting begins by SCRIBBLING. Every area of knowledge, whether it be agriculture, medicine or psychology, is the product of a long history of development. Should we expect human knowledge of right and wrong, or faith in God to be exempt from such progress?

Truly God is always communicating (revealing) his ways and nature to us, but that communication is 'filtered' through our imperfect understanding, emotions and words.

Jeremiah

Such is shown for example in the ministry of Jeremiah. We find the prophet in agony over his response to God's call to speak out against the immoral behaviour of the people of Judah, and to foretell its violent consequences. When the result fails to materialise quickly, Jeremiah is ridiculed and feels that even God has deceived him. *'You have duped me'*, he cries. *(Jeremiah 20.7)* But further reflection turned him to believe that God's call was genuine, and that he must renew his prophecy. He does so, only to find that he is opposed by another prophet, Hananiah, proclaiming, *'These are the words of the Lord of hosts, the God of Israel.' (28.2)* Jeremiah had said that the 'yoke' of the king of Babylon would be imposed upon his nation, Judah, but Hananiah prophesied that it would be broken. Both prophets believed that they were speaking 'God's Word'. One of them was wrong! Here we see the evidence of imperfection, even of those who would claim Divine revelation! Still, one of them could be right! And God perseveres in educating people, in spite of their frailty. (Read of Peter's learning in *Acts of the Apostles 10,* and Saul's growth in experience and faith in *Acts 9.)*

So, the Bible is a compilation of the developing response of imperfect people to the God who is 'speaking' to them. Then *we* who read their response have to assess their words by means of observation, reason, experience and prayer to God.

CONTRADICTIONS IN THE BIBLE

THE READER who starts with the first Book of the Bible, *Genesis,* will find two accounts of God's creation of the world. The first one tells us that human beings were made *after* the plants and animals. (Chapter 1) The second reverses that order (Chapter 2). Reason tells us that both cannot be accurate. The point being stressed here is not whether either account is scientifically accurate, but that such *contradictions* deny the claim that the Bible is infallible.

What sense can be made of two contradictory sentences from two prophets?

> *'They will beat their swords into mattocks and their spears into pruning-knives; nation will not lift sword against nation nor ever again be trained for war.' (Isaiah 2.4)*
>
> *'Beat your mattocks into swords and your pruning-knives into spears.' (Joel 3.10)*

Just one more instance -though countless more could be given- will suffice to endorse our point. The four Gospels each end with accounts of Jesus' resurrection. There is a discrepancy at the scene of the empty tomb: Mark tells of *'a young man sitting on the right side'*; Luke writes, *'two men stood... in dazzling apparel'*; Matthew states, *'an angel of the Lord... came and rolled back the stone, and sat upon it'*; John does not mention that anyone strange was there, only *'the stone had been moved away'.*

Which account is correct? Someone has either misheard the original witness, or elaborated it. Whichever way, we cannot say that each Gospel here is the 'Word of the all-knowing, infallible God'. Contrarily, they show the fallibility of the human Gospel authors.

These instances of contradiction are relatively unimportant, but other instances are crucial. The issue, for example, of our behaviour to people of other faiths or nationalities than ours *is* important. (Book Four, Part 1, p.4-8) The Bible gives conflicting answers. Jeremiah writing to his fellow Jews exiled in Babylon advises, *'Seek the welfare of any city to which I have exiled you, and pray to the Lord for it.' (Jeremiah 29.7)* However, Ezra back in Palestine exhorts the Jews: *'Let us now pledge ourselves to our God to get rid of all foreign wives with their children.' (Ezra 10.3)* Which of these attitudes accords with the 'mind of God'?

WRONG THEOLOGY IN THE BIBLE

AS well as contradictions we find wrong theology in certain passages. Here are some samples -

> *'I, the Lord your God, punish the children for the sins of the parents to the third and fourth generation of those who reject me.' (Exodus 20.5)*

Whilst it is often true that children suffer as a result of their parents' wrongdoing, it is wrong to assert that God's *intention* is to punish children for their parents' sin. This point is made elsewhere in the Bible *(Ezekiel 18.1-4)* (The subject of inherited punishment is just one aspect of the larger issue in the Bible of God as judge and punisher of our sin, to be treated in *Book Three, Part 1.)*

There is an account in *Genesis (22.1-18)* of the near-sacrifice by Abraham of his son, Isaac to God. Whilst it is true that life as a whole is a school of character, where there are difficult choices to be made -in a marriage or business, for example- it cannot be true that God would ask a human being to kill his son as a sacrifice to God. We must contrast this notion with Jesus' emphatic teaching of how God commends the care of a father for his son *(Matthew 7.7-11)*

The Israelites under Joshua believe that in response to God giving them victory over the city of Jericho, all the inhabitants of the city 'belong' to God and must be sacrificed/put to death *(Joshua 6 & 7).* Is that right Christian theology?

The prophet, Amos, believes that God manipulates nature in order to persuade people to do his will *(Amos 4.6-9).* I have reason to believe that God does not! As Minister of Newtown Church in St.Helens I arranged a number of summer outings. Each one had taken place in gorgeous weather, and remarks such as 'God looks after his own' and 'The sun shines on the righteous' were made! I responded with Jesus' saying, *'God causes the sun to rise on good and bad alike'.* God does not alter the forces of nature either to favour or to punish. This point was verified soon afterwards, when I arranged a Church trip to north Lancashire. A forecast of the deepest depression I have ever seen on TV was made on that morning. It materialised as we endured pouring rain and a force 9 gale, churning Morecambe Bay from shore to shore! So much for Divine manipulation!

WRONG ADVICE IN THE BIBLE

'AS in all congregations of God's people, women should keep silent in the meeting. They have no permission to talk, but should keep their place as the law directs' (1 Corinthians 14.33-4).

Paul's advice has denied the Church the resource of women's wisdom and enthusiasm for generations. This has also inhibited women's self-respect, and aided the subjugation of women by men.

We read in Matthew's Gospel; *'You must not think that I have come to bring peace to the earth, but a sword' (10.34).* This saying attributed to Jesus is often lifted out of context, and becomes wrong advice. Whilst Jesus' ways of loving and serving challenge all who hate and are self-serving, and so cause divisions, so often the saying is seen as a warrant for strife and war, or for the tolerance of such wrongs.

THE PROPER USE... AND THE MISUSE OF THE BIBLE

'IF the trumpet-call is not clear, who will prepare for battle? (1 Corinthians 14.8) It is often claimed that belief in an infallible Bible gives to the believer an instrument of certainty, a note of authority, especially contrasting him or her with the unclear, wishy-washy Bible-critic. However, when we survey the overall situation, we find the opposite to be true, because accepting infallibility means subscribing to contradictory beliefs about crucial issues - as we have already seen. This leads to confusion, lack of clear principle and even wrongdoing.

Slave trade in Bristol, 19th Century

Classic cases of this are -

- *'Slaves are to respect their masters' authority in everything... they will add lustre to the doctrine of God our saviour.' (Letter to Titus 2.9,10).* How slavers would find Bible-justification for their practice over the centuries!
- *The Letter to the Romans (1.27)* named homosexuality as a *'perversion'*, leading to the persecution of people with a natural condition to this day.
- Should we hate people or love them? - See conflicting answers in *Psalm 139.22; Ecclesiastes 3.8; Matthew 5.43-8*
- Is our attitude to God to be fear or love? Read *Deuteronomy 13.4; Revelation 14.17; Romans 8.15 and 1 John 4.18* - Confused?
- Should a disciple of Jesus remain celibate or get married, preferably? - *1 Corinthians 7.32-3* advises celibacy, whilst *Mark 10.6,7* commends marriage.

How many people have gone through near agony trying to follow confusing and sometimes wrong-headed authority!

But what is the proper use of the Bible? - *It is an honest attempt to sift out the right from the wrong in every 'book' of the Bible and every passage.* This is the theme of the last section of this Part.

BIBLE CRITICISM IS OUR KEY TO THE BIBLE

OUR consideration of the imperfections of the Bible - alongside its virtues - very much illustrates the dilemma of many, nurtured in the Christian Church. May not the same be true of Jews and Moslems with their Scriptures?

The Bible-critic will be challenged: 'If the Bible is so flawed, surely you are like a seafarer without chart or compass! Also you have rendered the Bible as a "lame-duck" scripture; a hit-and-miss guide to life!' How can we deal with such aspersions?

- *Hit-and-miss?* No, it is insistence on the unquestionable Bible with its confusions, wrong theology and misleading advice which is 'hit-and-miss'.
- *No chart and compass?* Certainly the Bible-critic *does* have a chart and compass. They consist of eyes, reason, experience, prayer, and the ever-living-and-communicating God's revelation of the truth. *'God has not left himself without some clue to his nature.' (Acts 14.17)* Here is quoted a sentence from the Bible which the author does believe to be true(!) because its words agree with experience.

- God 'talks' to every generation; to people in 'Bible-times' -and to us today - through observation of nature, *'God's book',* for example, reason and revelation.

These arguments of this author are supported eloquently by the Rev.W.Dorling writing in the Essex Congregational Magazine (June 1874):

> *'I am proud and thankful to be able to think for myself. I am far more concerned to know what there is in my "breast" than what those good men thought and felt two or three hundred years ago.*
> *The living thoughts of our hearts today are dearer to us than the greatest thoughts of departed worthies.*
> *... Behind all creeds and councils stands in simple, solemn, separate majesty the solitary human soul. To that God speaks; with that he has communion; to that he leaves responsibility for dealing with his truths... God can trust his truth to the mind which he has created.'*

'Freethinking', then, is one element in our *'chart and compass'.*

Think on these words of John Locke in his 'Essay concerning Human Understanding':

'GOD would have us use the discerning faculties he has given us.'

And these of William Chillingworth in 'The Religion of Protestants. A Safe way to Salvation':

'I am certain that God hath given us our reason to discern truth and falsehood.'

Thought and reason, then, are useful guides to life. So is EXPERIENCE. *'Experience is the best teacher'*, said a respected Primary School Headteacher in Preston, Lancashire. As we work for God in the care and service of people, we learn more about God and his purposes. We gain in action what Michael Taylor, sometime Principal of the Northern Baptist College, called *'intrinsic authority'*. Such authority is held by a surgeon. His knowledge is not only from a textbook; it is in his hands and in his mind.

The last-but-not-least element in our 'chart and compass' is OBSERVATION. Just as we learn so much about a human being from seeing his or her works -a painting or a novel or a sailing ship so we may trace the character of God from nature, God's creation. This truth was finely expressed by John Keble's hymn:

'There is a book, who runs may read,
which heavenly truth imparts,
and all the lore its scholars need,
pure eyes and Christian hearts.'
'The works of God above, below,
within us and around,
are pages in that book to show how
God himself is found.'

CONCLUSION:
THE BOON OF SCRIPTURE CRITICISM

A FELLOW-MINISTER once deplored to me the 'crass ignorance' which he found in so many people. Too many people in his view don't bother to seek the truth or think for themselves: *'There are none so blind as those who will not see!'*

Thus, when we read the Bible without querying, we are at least naive, and in grave danger of missing the 'gold' among the 'dross'. Constructive questioning however leads us to the most valuable passages of the Bible, and steers us away from unhelpful ones.

We may end this quest for the source of knowledge about God and life with a fine expression of the search, as far as the Bible is concerned. It is found in the *'Basis of the Nature, Faith and Order of the United Reformed Church; Statement of Faith':*

'WE believe that the Word of God in the Old and New Testaments,

discerned under the guidance of the Holy Spirit,
is the supreme authority for the faith and conduct of all God's people.'

The key phrase in this quotation is *'discerned under the guidance of the Holy Spirit'*. As we study the Bible we have to *discern/sift out*, by means of observation, reason, experience and prayer, the genuine Word of God from the fallible human notions, both of which the Bible contains.

Our conclusion, then, is that freethinking and Bible-believing need not by themselves be the only option: rather, we hold the two in balance, because they need each other.

Indeed, every Bible should have words such as these written prominently on its cover:

> THE BIBLE
> This book comes from the wealth of Divine-human relations.
> Be Prepared to sort out the 'Gold' from the 'Dross'.
> But be ready to find the truth here that will inspire you, and save you, and bring you into God's presence.

MAKING SENSE OF LIFE - BOOK TWO

THE MISSION AND MESSAGE OF JESUS

Part One

God - Lover and Saviour of the Human Soul

Human society as the Kingdom of God

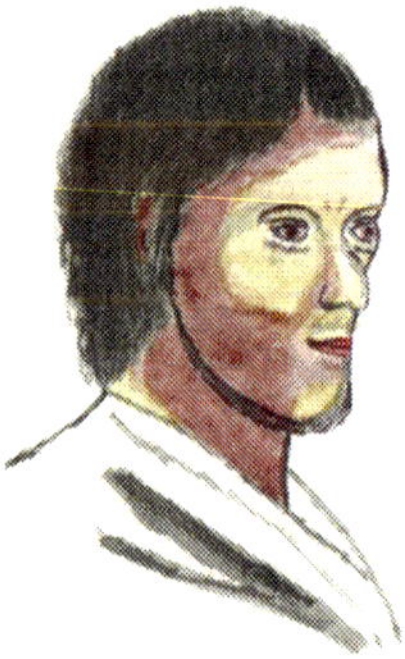

JESUS

God loves each human soul

Andrew - Disciple

Jesus befriends Zaccheus - superintendent of Roman taxes and ostracised by the strictly religious

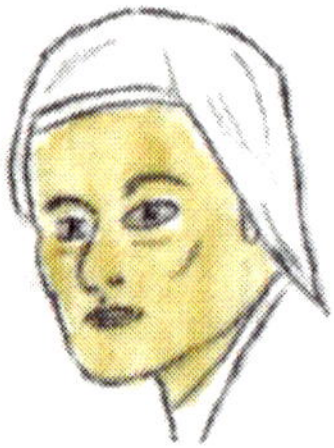

Mary Magdalene - healed by Jesus

'GOD could not be everywhere; therefore he made mothers.'

(Jewish Proverb)

GOD, is the Personal Creator of the universe, as we argued in *Book One, Part 2,* and as for humankind in that universe we may call God the *'ancestor'* of every human being.

Yet for the birth of every human child God provides a human mother. The life which comes from God in the first place proceeds immediately from a mother's womb. The new-born baby is not cradled in God's, but in a human female's arms; the infant depends on God's overall providence, but immediately on the mother's milk for sustenance of the body. And for love? Truly underneath is God's everlasting care, but again immediately and vitally the child receives love from the mother: especially through her eyes. Frank Lake, in his notes on *'Clinical Theology'* explains (right).

Access to the SIGHT of mother is access to life - to knowledge of who I am. The infants being lives in the light of her countenance. The LOOK in mother's eyes (and the SoUND of her voice) create belongingness.

So many faculties and the spirit, which God intends for each of us, are mediated to us through another human being, a mother.

THE LOVE OF GOD IN THE HUMAN LIFE OF JESUS

THE PURPOSE of this *Book* is to show that God's best gifts to us, both inwardly/individually and outwardly/socially, are mediated to us through the human JESUS. The apostle Paul put it like this –

"You see the glory (presence) of God in the face of Jesus Christ" (2 Corinthians 4.6)

DRAWING JESUS' PORTRAIT

IF Paul is correct, then it is vital that we do our best to draw the 'portrait' of Jesus as accurately as we can. It may be argued by those who believe in the infallibility of the Bible, that there is no need for you or I to try to 'portray' Jesus, because it is already there in the four New Testament Gospels, Matthew, Mark, Luke and John. Yet truthfully the case is that the gospels share the Bible's imperfections already noted in *Book One, Part 3.* We must then, before drawing our word-picture, explain briefly the Gospels' shortcomings, and how, in spite of them, we can paint as accurate a portrait as possible, given our own imperfections!

THE FIRST SKETCHES OF JESUS BEFORE THE GOSPELS

HOW were the Gospels written? This question has led to the most careful and detailed study in the 20th century. The results seem summarily to be as follows:

Jesus' public life was an activity of showing God's love by befriending people, healing those sick in body, mind and spirit, and teaching and gathering folk into communities of faith and mutual care. This activity lasted for something less than two years around the period of 30 AD.

Jesus made no written account of his brief career, wrote no autobiography, and left no textbook of his teaching. However, as the years proceeded after his earthly life people who were impressed and affected by his deeds and words started to record them.

The attempt to uncover these first records has recently been the project of the 'Jesus Seminar', a group of North American scholars. John Dominic Crossan is one of these whose writings seem to this author to be specially enlightening.

The 'Jesus Seminar' believe the first records to be the collections of the *teachings* of Jesus, produced about 20 to 30 years after Jesus' ministry. They are found in early editions of the so-called *'Gospels according to Thomas and the Hebrews'*, together with fragments of sayings of Jesus written on papyri, discovered in Egypt as late as the end of the 19th century. Beside these, study of the New Testament Gospels has led scholars to believe that *they* contain sections, which were 'sayings of Jesus' collections. Was Luke referring to this when he wrote in his Gospel:

> *'Many writers have undertaken to draw up an account of the events that have taken place among us, following the traditions handed down to us by the original eyewitnesses and servants of the gospel.' (Luke 1.1,2)?*

These collections themselves had a history of development according to the 'Jesus Seminar', who believe also that they reveal Jesus as his first followers knew him, and that this portrait has important differences from that of the authors of the later Four Gospels.

This belief seems to be well-based in that by and large the nearer we are to an incident or saying the more accurate the record will be. As time goes by memory tends to fade and more people bring their own ideas and purposes which can distort or overlay the originals.

THE WRITING OF THE NEW TESTAMENT GOSPELS

WHEN we read the New Testament Gospels we can see how they have set down the '*sayings* of Jesus collections' beside accounts of Jesus' *activity,* coming to a climax in Jesus' final conflict with those who opposed and eventually crucified him.

But the Gospel-authors did more. The Gospels are a distinct type of literature. They were written to proclaim the *'good news'* of what God had done through the earthly life, death and risen life of Jesus, and to encourage

Contents of a New Testament Gospel	
Collections of sayings *e.g. Matthew 5 - 7*	*Collections of activities* *e.g. Matthew 8 & 9*

people to accept God's help. Each Gospel, within this purpose, has a distinct vocabulary, style and composition, but more importantly each has a particular theology and target:

MATTHEW intends to present Jesus as delivering, like Moses, a new Divine teaching and instruction for the community, the Church, which he founded.

MARK explicitly sets out to proclaim Jesus as the 'Messiah', the one anointed by God as King, who inaugurates the 'Kingdom of God' on earth as it triumphs over demonic forces.

LUKE is distinct as being the former of a two-part writing (Acts of the Apostles being the latter), designed to commend Jesus as God's appointed saviour of all humankind.

JOHN aims to demonstrate that Jesus 'puts flesh' on God's original plan to impart to people a fuller life of happiness and truthfulness. This demonstration consisted of Jesus' remarkable 'signs' (miracles) and Divinely authoritative teaching.

Whilst the Gospels are novel, they employ some traditional literary forms, which it is useful to note:

- the form of Hellenistic Greek biography written to dispel a false image of their subject and to provide a true model for the readers.
- the form of Socratic question-and-answer dialogue.
- the form of Jewish *Haggadah*, interpreting the narrative and theological sections of their scriptures.
- the form of apocalyptic, that is, claims to record revelations or visions about the Divine realm and the future course of history.
- the form of aretology, that is, accounts of miracles of a god or semi-divine hero.

Such are the New Testament Gospels.

A GOSPEL BEFORE THE GOSPELS

IT seems to be the case according to the 'Jesus Seminar' that the purpose and the theological belief of the Four Gospels, together with their use of the forms of writing just listed, have overlaid and to varied extents distorted the historical Jesus. But he can be more clearly portrayed when we uncover the earliest collections of his sayings.

Burton L. Mack, one of the members of the 'Jesus Seminar', in *'The Lost Gospel'*, notes the absence from the earliest layer or source of Jesus' collected sayings, known as *'Q'* (from the German, *'quelle'* = 'source'), of any belief, typical of the Four Gospels, that Jesus was the *'Messiah'*; no condemnation of Judaism; no mention of the crucifixion as a tragic or saving event planned by God; no worship or honour of Jesus as God; no formation of a religious cult; nor any extensive mission to Jews or Gentiles.

These omissions tell the negative aspect of the earliest known writings of Jesus' followers, but they have a positive side. They tell, as Mack writes, of a *'vigorous Jesus movement'*, and of *'factors other than belief that Jesus was Divine, which played a role in the generation of early Jesus and Christ movements'.* They indeed form the basis of what the present author believes to be as accurate a portrait of Jesus as we can find, and which is just as much 'good news' for us today as it was for the people Jesus lived with and loved, as evidenced in his earliest sayings. (See page 47-48).

Furthermore, close study of the sayings-collections by John Kloppenborg of the Institute of Antiquity & Christianity at Claremont in the USA identified three layers or editions of *'Q'*, embedded in *Matthew* and *Luke*:

(Q1) consists of wise sayings of Jesus.
(Q2) announces judgement on adversaries of Jesus' movement.
(Q3) is a small amount of material of varied nature.

The first layer would seem to be at the heart of Jesus' 'good news'.

JESUS AND HIS GOOD NEWS

WHAT then is Jesus' 'good news/gospel'? Here is a parable:

The door-bell rings. Mrs. Brown goes and opens up. A policeman stands there. He brings *bad* news.

'Mrs. Brown?' he enquires.

'Yes.'

'I'm afraid your son has been swept overboard from his ship. He is missing.'

Mrs. Brown is in a state of shock... But three hours later the 'phone rings, and the caller says,

'Good news, Mrs. Brown. It's the police. Your son has been picked up alive by the lifeboat. He's safe.'

GOOD NEWS. These words are virtually the theme of the mission and message of Jesus. So much so, that the documents that narrate the life and teaching of Jesus are called 'good news' – 'Gospel'.

'Good news' is indeed the guide to convey us through the 'thicket' of the often confusing Gospels, and *Mark* introduces the ministry of Jesus with the statement: *'Jesus came into Galilee proclaiming the GOOD NEWS OF GOD.' (1.14)*

Like Mrs. Brown in our short story, *GOOD NEWS* is what so many of us – in every age – so desperately want to hear, because as the book of *Job* so ruefully observes: *'Man is born to trouble as surely as sparks shoot upwards.' (Job 5.7)*

THE GOOD NEWS – GOD CARES ABOUT YOU

MANY PEOPLE in Jesus' Galileean and Judaean communities were in trouble. *'My son was lost!'* explains a father in Jesus' parable. A son left home to seek a good time, but sank into deep trouble. (A situation not unknown in our 21st century!) His eventual return home and his father's pardon opened up a bitter rift between him and the brother still at home. Jesus knew such meshes of broken relationships with their entail of lovelessness, loneliness and guilt. He may well have probed inside the human soul, and heard the anguished questions: *'Is there any love in this life; anyone who cares; has life a meaning?'* These questions must have been asked by another soul in trouble: a woman in a state of prolonged and painful menstruation. She was pronounced 'ceremonially unclean', and her normal relations with society were broken. She also knew lovelessness, loneliness, meaninglessness and guilt. Another tormented soul was *'a woman who was living an immoral life'*, a prostitute, but who came to feel ashamed of her behaviour, her loveless relationships, and her need to be truly in love.

What was Jesus' 'good news' for people like these? It was, as *Mark* put it, *'good news of God'*. When the human soul is stripped of every bodily comfort and bereft of every human friend, is there *anyone* to comfort or befriend or forgive you?

'YES THERE IS!' is Jesus' reply. This *anyone* is THE PERSONAL GOD, our Maker, Father and Friend! Here is the evidence:

> *'Very early next morning Jesus got up and went out,' Mark records (1.35)*
> *'He went away to a remote spot and remained there in prayer.'*

Jesus knew what it was like to be alone with God, in a 'one-to-one' encounter. And what kind of God did Jesus meet?

Here are some extracts from the *core* of Jesus' teaching – the sayings-collection, *'Q1'*.

> *Would any of you offer his son a stone when he*
> *asks for bread, or a snake when he asks for a fish?*
> *If you, bad as you are, know how to give good gifts to your children,*
> *how much more will your heavenly Father*
> *give good things to those who ask him.'*
> *(Matthew 7.9-11)*
> *'Are not two sparrows sold for a penny?*
> *Yet without your Father's knowledge*
> *not one of them can fall to the ground.*
> *As for you, even the hairs of your head have all been counted,*

so do not be afraid; you are worth more
than any number of sparrows.'
(Matthew 10.29-31)
'Your heavenly Father causes the sun to rise
on good and bad alike, and sends the rain
on the innocent and the wicked.'
(Matthew 5.45)

The God with whom Jesus converses is One who cherishes each person; One whose goodwill is to be trusted; One who, because he cherishes, is not vindictive, but – as we reasoned in *Book One, Part 2* – is generous, patient and merciful.

The Belgian theologian, Edward Schillebeeckx, in his book, *'Jesus'*, concludes his study of *'The Gospel of Jesus Christ'* with this summary:

> *'Jesus proclaimed the rule of God, oriented on humanity... He identifies himself in person with the cause of God as that also of man... human beings are people whom God cherishes.'*

'HANDSOME IS AS HANDSOME DOES'

TEACHING, of course, *can* be just empty words! But in Jesus' case his action is four-square with his teaching. Cleopas, an early follower, testifies: *'About Jesus of Nazareth, who by deeds and words of power proved himself a prophet in the sight of God and the whole people.' (Luke 24.19)*

God's cherishing, goodwill and mercy shine through the *deeds* of Jesus as we read the Gospels.

So, we see a man coming to Jesus who has a dreaded skin disease. He has been ostracised and is lonely. He asks Jesus to touch and heal him. Jesus does so, risking condemnation by taboo-minded people; but he is more concerned for the man in his need. *(Mark 1.40-5)*

A paralysed man, who with others assumed his illness was a Divine punishment for some wrong-doing, is brought to Jesus, who tells the man that God has forgiven his sins. He is released from his guilt – and his paralysis.

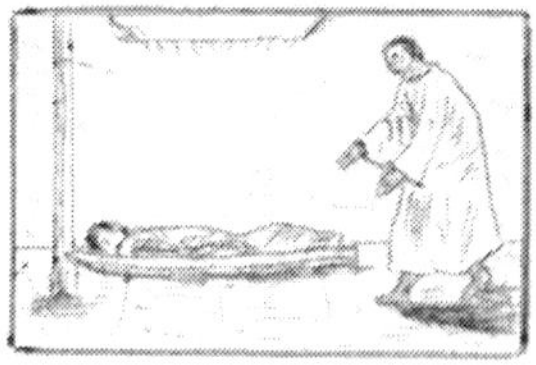

> *'Jesus says to the paralysed man, "Your sins are forgiven".' (Mark 2.9)*

A man, sick in mind and convinced as countless others were that he was ruled by an 'unclean spirit' or 'demon' was in the same synagogue-congregation as Jesus. He shouted: *'Have you come to destroy us? I know who you are –the Holy One of God.'*

Jesus knew the unrivalled power and goodness of God – as he recalled his Scripture: *'You shall do homage to the Lord your God and worship him alone.'*

The man then had nothing to fear: God alone, the God of pure righteousness, who cared for him, was to be respected and trusted. The 'demon' was overcome; it *'left him.' (Mark 1.23-6)*

So, no man or woman however flawed is worthless to Jesus – or to God. God cherishes them!

Mark, thus, recounts this incident:

> *'Many tax-collectors and sinners were seated with Jesus and his disciples, for there were many of them among his followers. Some scribes who were Pharisees, observing the company in which he was eating, said to his disciples, "Why does he eat with tax-collectors and sinners?" Hearing this, Jesus said to them, "It is not the healthy who need a doctor, but the sick; I did not come to call the virtuous, but sinners".' (Mark 2.15-17)*

THE '*WHITE-HEAT*' OF GOD'S LOVE

THE teaching and actions of Jesus, here cited, are the core of his mind and soul, of his activity, and of his *good news of God* – to the individual.

E. P. Sanders, the American scholar of Jesus and Judaism, in *'The Historical Figure of Jesus',* sums up Jesus' stance: *'He was not given to censure but to encouragement; he was not judgmental but compassionate and lenient.'*

Jesus indeed experienced in the centre of his being the pure infinite love, moral goodness, mercy and patience of GOD: what we may call the *'white-heat of God's love'*. This intense 'heat'- love – was conveyed by Jesus like a lightning conductor, to people. It was this which warmed, comforted, cheered and inspired many whom Jesus met; it was the love, compassion and mercy which attracted men and women to Jesus as friends, disciples and apostles (messengers to others). This was true in Palestine nearly 2000 years ago – and has been so over the centuries to this day!

THE CONSISTENT GOD

THERE is a consequence, important for our theology and life, of our assessment of Jesus' core message. It concerns *consistency.* Not only ought words and deeds to be consistent, but a person's innermost character must be consistent, harmonious, integrated. An inconsistent person, a 'man of moods', is an unreliable menace. How much more a 'God of moods', now merciful, then vengeful! Jesus' teaching here is unambiguous. He shows by word and deed a *TOTALLY LOVING, MORALLY-GOOD AND MERCIFUL GOD:* the opposite of wrathful and vindictive. We can alone rely on and *make sense* of a God who is *consistent in character.* Such is Jesus' God. So, the good-for-nothing son in Jesus' story is welcomed home by his father – if not by his brother. The father pleads, *'This son of mine was dead and has come back to life; he was lost and is found.' (Luke 15.24)*

Yet someone said recently, 'I think of God as stern, severe, judgmental, wrathful; whereas Jesus is compassionate and merciful.' Nothing could be further from the truth! As there is no 'split-personality' in God, there is no discrepancy between the character of God and the message of Jesus.

Jesus forgives and God forgives. That is the core of Jesus' mission and message.

> Perhaps the greatest question religious people have to answer is:
> DOES GOD FORGIVE OR DOES HE NOT?

This point is vital. When we recall our notice of the inconsistencies in the Bible as a whole *(Book One, Part 3)*, involving human notions about God's character, it is so important that , if by our best efforts we have discovered the core of Jesus' teaching about God, we must make this the yardstick of the truth of every statement in the Bible and elsewhere.

We should note here some statements (references) in the Old Testament which harmonise with the core of Jesus' message-

Hosea 11.1-9; Isaiah 6.1-7; Jeremiah 31.31-4;
Ezekiel 33.10,11; Isaiah 40.1-11; Psalm 103.1-14

Here is a recurring message of God's patience and mercy. God condemns our wrongdoing, but always has mercy on us.

OUR '*HOT-LINE*' TO GOD

THERE is another consequence of the love between God and us. We are in a personal, intimate and direct relation to God. It seems that Jesus used the intimate Jewish word *'abba', 'Father',* when he prayed to God. *(Mark 14.36)* Paul indicates that early Christians did the same: they are able to *'cry "abba, Father!" (Romans 8.15)* We can say in 21st century parlance that we have a *'hot-line'* to God. We can pray directly to God without any intermediary or broker as Jesus taught us:

'FATHER, your name be hallowed; your kingdom come.
Give us each day our daily bread.
And forgive us our sins, for we too forgive all who have done us wrong.
And do not put us to the test.' (Luke 11.2-4)

RELAX!

ONE of the most profound differences that Jesus' good news made to the lives of those who received it was a trust in God's cherishing and care, and in God's forgiveness of wrong thoughts and deeds. This helped them to *relax* in God's presence. Their burdens of guilt, shame and fear were lifted from them; they were no longer 'uptight' and miserable.

Evidence in the Gospels seems to show this fact:

'Once, when John's disciples and the Pharisees were keeping a fast, some people came and asked Jesus, "Why is it that John's disciples and the disciples of the Pharisees are fasting, but yours are not?" He replied,

"Can you expect the bridegroom's friends to fast while the bridegroom is with them." ' (Mark 2.18-19)

Fasting is frequently associated with lamentation and penance for sin. So, *'The Israelites, clothed in sackcloth and with dust on their heads, assembled for a fast.' (Nehemiah 9.1)* Penance has its place; admission of guilt is essential for moral growth – as is conversion to goodness. But, that done, the soul must progress to glad acceptance of God's love and mercy. It is like a wedding; a time of joyful loving; the bridegroom and his friends should be happy and *relaxed!* God now loves us, 'warts and all': he wants us to be calm, trusting and joyful.

Edward Schillebeeckx sums up Jesus' spirit concisely in his Book, *'Jesus': 'Being sad in Jesus' presence is an existential impossibility.'*

WHO WAS JESUS?

JESUS was clearly a remarkable person, and had a close relationship with God. Very early in the history of the Church we read Peter's proclamation to a crowd in Jerusalem:

'Men of Israel, hear me: I am speaking of Jesus of Nazareth, a man (Greek, "andra") singled out by God..' (Acts of the Apostles2.22)

Here Jesus was not looked on as being Divine or semi-Divine., but plainly as a human being - *a man.* Indeed the earliest disciples seem to have regarded him as a *prophet.* We recall the opinion of Cleopas *(Luke 24.19),* and the Pharisees considered whether he was such: *'If this man were a real prophet..'* (Luke 7.39).

Quite soon, however, followers, especially those with Jewish or Hellenistic Greek religious knowledge, began to believe that Jesus fitted into their conceptions or faith-categories. So, he was seen as *'Messiah-Christ';* or *'Son of God';* or *'Lord',* a title variously applied to Jehovah-God or to a highly-respected person; or *'The Word (Greek, 'Logos') of God',* God's Plan in human flesh.

Christians by the 4th century were sure that Jesus was Divine, writing in the Nicene creed:

'We believe in... one Lord Jesus Christ... true God of true God, begotten not made, of one substance with (God) the Father, through whom all things were made...'

Isaac Watts, the 18th century hymn-writer, in *'When I survey the wondrous cross...* ' sings of *'Christ my God'.* The 20th century Christian songwriter, Graham Kendrick, in his song about Jesus, *'Meekness and majesty',* calls him, *'The man who is God'.* All this is, to say the least, paradoxical. Is it rational? Can Jesus be man and God at the same time? There is room for interpretation when Ministers in the United Reformed Church confess their belief that:

'Jesus Christ... living our human life among us... is God's gift of himself to the world..'

Who then was Jesus? The apostle Peter says he was *'a man singled out by God'.* Graham Kendrick says he was *'the man who is God'.* Man or God, which?

Further reading of the New Testament will help our quest. A significant passage is Mark's description of Jesus' crisis in the garden of Gethsemane, where he is faced with the decision whether to continue his mission and face death or to abandon it and spare his life. He prays:

> *'Abba Father, all things are possible to you; take this cup from me. Yet not my will but yours.' (Mark 14.36)*

The plain understanding of this incident is that one person, Jesus, is speaking to another person, the Father, God. Is it not then against common sense - against reason - to say that Jesus *is* God?

What then is reason's answer to the query, *'Who was Jesus?'*

JESUS WAS A MAN WHO WAS INTIMATE WITH GOD

We may now well ask, *How did Jesus come into this intimate relationship with God?*

We unfortunately know little about the early development of Jesus. We should dearly like to know more about his background of family, education and career. We can, taking it that he was fully human, surmise that he grew in knowledge of human life and in communion with God within the same restrictions and opportunities shared by his fellow men, women and children. The Gospels reveal Jesus' awareness of people's desires and hopes, fears and temptations. Had he not shared them? His emphasis on trust in God, compassion and forgiveness would lead us to suppose the probability that he knew what it was like to do wrong, feel guilty, and long to be forgiven; to experience condemnation, fear of the devil, prevalent in his society, and doubt of God's goodness and power. All in all, we may presume that Jesus could help and save lonely, troubled, guilty and despairing people because he had been there HIMSELF! We cannot prove this, but we can have a strong hunch of it!

We can also deduce that Jesus was aided on the way to knowledge and experience of the Personal God by his acquaintance with the Jewish Scriptures taught to him as a boy in the synagogue at Nazareth.

A synongogue school

He would also have held conversations with religious people, and made his own observation of nature and human life. He would have reflected on all this and shared it with God in prayer. All these sources brought him to that intimate, direct relationship with God, which we have seen it was his passion to make real for everyone who could listen and seek.

Jesus, then, in a sentence, was a fully human being who was intimate with God, and was called to bring God close to everyone.

This conclusion leads is to the final point of this *Part*.

PROCLAIM THE GOOD NEWS!

THE mission and message of Jesus which brought God's love, healing and salvation to people, who often were bitter or despairing or full of hate, Jesus' ministry of Divine-human reconciliation, spurred those same people to pass on the message to others. They became in J. D. Crossan's phrase *'healed healers'*. Moreover, that is what Jesus called them to be and to do.

He said

'Nothing is hidden that will not be made known,
or secret that will not come to light.
What I tell you in the dark, speak in the light.
And what you hear as a whisper, proclaim on the housetops.'
(Matthew 10.27)

The Personal God, Creator of the universe, and Lover and Saviour, thus cares for everyone in this world. That care shone *'in the face of Jesus Christ'*, and it is in that sense that we can endorse Paul's affirmation in *2 Corinthians 5.19*

'GOD was in Christ
reconciling the world to himself,
no longer holding people's misdeeds against them and has
ENTRUSTED US WITH THE MESSAGE OF RECONCILIATION.'
JESUS chose companions, and sent them out
to proclaim the gospel.

THIS is how the Christian mission began and has continued for almost 2000 years!

MAKING SENSE OF LIFE - BOOK TWO

THE MISSION AND MESSAGE OF JESUS

Part Two

Human Society & The Kingdom of God

HUMAN SOCIETY IN JESUS' PALESTINE

Winnowing corn for 'daily bread'.

A Galilean village community

Lake Galilee's thriving fisheries put much 'bread' on the table

A society overseen by the Roman Empire

'NO man is an Iland, intire of it selfe; every man is a peece of the Continent, I am involved in Mankinde; and therefore never send to know for whom the bell tolls; It tolls for Thee.'
(John Donne.17th Century)

A much earlier Hebrew poet wrote:

'God gives the friendless a home.' (Psalm 68.6)

And in the Hebrew creation-parable God says of the first man, Adam:

'It is not good for the man to be alone: I will provide a partner for him.' (Genesis 2.18)

God's eternal plan involves both human individuals and society.

TROUBLE AND STRIFE

TRAGICALLY human weakness and selfishness have 'put a spoke' into the Divine plan. We shall observe and assess the reasons for evil in *Book Three, Part 1,* but by one means or another so much of human society has endured appalling trouble

Jesus was born into a troubled society. J. D. Crossan paints the scene vividly in his book, *'Jesus, a Revolutionary Biography'*. He records that 95-97% of people were illiterate; the majority were peasants; only 5% were tradesmen; those who were tenant-farmers yielded 2/3 of their crops to the upper classes, and were just that much better than the many unemployed and destitute people who were forced to beg. Meanwhile the ruling elite, 1% of the population, were extremely rich, owning over 50% of the country just ahead of their retainers, the priests and merchants, who owned another 15% of the land...

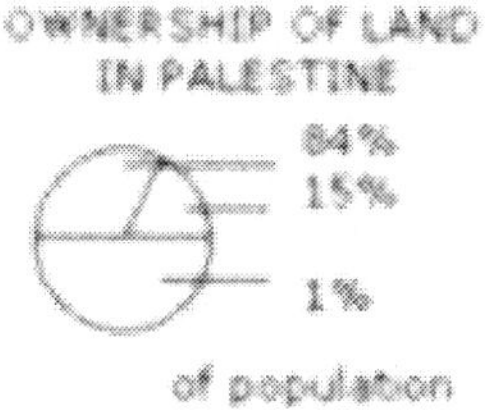

It takes little imagination to envisage the volume of suffering and misery endured by very many people because of this maldistribution of resources. Jesus encountered day after day destitute beggars and folk *'suffering from various diseases'. (Mark 1.34)* He saw victims of leprosy, serious skin-diseases, dropsy, paralysis, blindness, deafness, fevers, lameness; not to mention multifarious types of mental illness and anguish.

Nor might we be so myopic to miss the resentment, sullen or blazing, felt by those who realised the unjust gulf between the plutocrats and the destitute - as this Gospel-parable of Jesus shows:

'There was once a rich man, who used to dress in purple and the finest linen, and feasted sumptuously every day. At his gate lay a poor man named Lazarus, who was covered with sores. He would have been glad

to satisfy his hunger with scraps from the rich man's table. Dogs used to come and lick his sores. (Luke 16. 19-21)

Furthermore, desperate poverty, then as now, often led people into burglary and brigandage - as with Barabbas.

Then, pressing down on this basic level of trouble was the heavy weight of imperial oppression. Crossan quotes Calgacus, a rebel-general against Rome, c. 80 AD:

'To plunder, butcher, steal; these things they misname "empire": they make a desolation and call it "peace".'

A particularly cruel instance in Palestine was the crucifixion of 2000 Jewish rebels by the Roman governor of Syria, Varus, in 4 BC.

God's plan for society was spoiled; the ground-rules of community - no murder, adultery, theft, giving false evidence, coveting- were continually broken. Society was over and again torn apart - male against female, parent against child, Jew versus Samaritan - and Roman and Greek, and most of all, as already noted, rich against poor. Could a broken human society be mended?

THE KINGDOM OF GOD...
AND THE MINISTRY OF TROUBLE-SHOOTING

WE put the question in *Part 1* of this *Book* in reference to personal troubles of body and soul; *'Is there any love in this life? Is there anyone who cares?'*

Jesus had a definite answer: 'YES, the Personal God, the Creator of all, cares about every human being.'

Jesus is every bit as definite about God's care for *society*, that is, folk living together. This care he calls *'the kingdom of God'.* God's care for society 'God's people'- had been acknowledged by Jesus' nation at least from the time of Moses. Divine concern about social matters such as justice and peace had been the theme of liberators, kings and prophets.- Now we shall show how Jesus made that concern his mission and message.

THE KINGDOM OF GOD IS HERE AND NOW

'FATHER... your kingdom come.' (Luke 11.2) These words from Jesus' prayer are now known around the earth. But what do they mean? Are Jesus' disciples expecting the prayer to be answered *today,* or in the distant future?

The answer is found when we compare Jesus' view of the 'kingdom of God' with that of John the Baptist. Whilst John, like Jesus, called for a fair distribution of material goods *'Whoever has two shirts must share with him who has none.'*

(Luke 3.10) for John this was an interim measure, pending God's *'coming retribution' (Matthew 3.7)*. God is going to intervene in humankind's sad and wayward history to punish wrong and set life straight. John's view, says Crossan, is: *'We wait for God to act'*

Jesus saw it differently. Crossan again interprets Jesus: *'God waits for us to act.'* God enacts the policy of his kingdom -his righting of injustice, healing of the sick and reconciling of enemies- *through us human beings, HERE AND NOW:* not in 'the sweet-by-and-by'! A. E. Harvey writes in 'Jesus and the Constraints of History':

Two Views of Life in a Nutshell
John the Baptist - *"We will wait for God to act."*
Jesus - *"God waits for us to act."*

> *'Jesus' teaching has an altogether more urgent tone... he proclaimed the imminence and actuality (of better things)... he did not merely use the word "kingdom" as a way of talking about the eternal sovereignty of God, but proclaimed it as an imminent reality.'*

Jesus says (Crossan's translation):

> *'The Kingdom of God comes not at some future time:*
> *You cannot point out the sign of its coming.*
> *The Kingdom of God comes not at some special site:*
> *You cannot point out the place of its coming.*
> *The Kingdom of God is already here, among you, now.'*
> *(Matthew 24.23-6)*

SUCH was the conviction of Jesus and his passion and mission. Let us see now how it was worked out in the various aspects of the society he lived in.

PARENTS AND CHILDREN

THE basic unit of society is the *family* - the 'nuclear' family of parents and children. The breakdown in the family unit in 1st century Palestine consisted in the abused power of the parents, especially the father. He could rule tyrannically over the body, mind and soul of his wife and children. Thus, whilst a parent could bequeath good traits and habits to the children, bad habits and prejudices could be perpetuated from one generation to another, and the possibility of improvement in knowledge and behaviour could be suffocated. Jesus' attitude of respect for the dignity of each human being challenged such tyranny. Each person had a right to choose between good and bad for himself or herself; not just to repeat ancestral ways.

Yet, the older generation often prefers the 'old wine' *(Luke 5.39),* and pours scorn on any new - and better - ways. *Luke 11.27-8* records (trans. Crossan):

> *'Out of the crowd a woman shouted, "Fortunate the womb that bore you, the breasts that nursed you."*

Back to the woman Jesus replied:

> *"Fortunate the ears that hear the word of God, the will that obeys the word of God".'*

Respect and honour from child to father and mother remained, but that attitude should work both ways. It is sad when it does not. Hence Jesus' words (trans. Crossan) in *(Matthew 10.34-6):*

One Generation to the Next
Parents' legacy to their children

GOOD	BAD
Love	Hatred
Honesty	Lying
Patience	Irritability
Diligence	Laziness
Tolerance	Prejudice

> *'The kingdom of God divides the household, three against two, two against three, father against son, son against father, mother against daughter, daughter against mother...'*

Jesus commended the caring father, as we have noted, but peace between the generations could not exist at the price of parental abuse and tyranny.

MALE AND FEMALE

> *'O GOD, I thank you that I was not born a Gentile, a slave or a WOMAN!'*

Such was a prayer of Jews in the 1st century. A letter from the same time, unearthed at Oxyrhynchus, Egypt, read: *'Hilarion to his wife, "If by chance you bear a son, let it be; if it is a girl, cast it out (to die)."'* Crossan comments: *'A child is a nobody, unless the father accepted it as a member of the family.'*

The rights of a wife were few.

> *'Though she did much of the hard work, she had a low position, being owned by her husband, and looking up to him as her master.'*
> *('Family Encyclopedia of the Bible')*

Jesus' conviction and teaching about the worth of the individual person, again, was the basis of his attitude to man-woman relations. His compassion on those in trouble clearly applied both to women and men.

> *'A number of women who had been set free (by Jesus) from evil spirits and infirmities... provided (for Jesus and his disciples) out of their own resources.'*
> *(Luke 8.2,3)*

Luke also records an incident where Mary, sister of Martha, listens to Jesus as he teaches. Jesus commends her for this, clearly signaling that a woman - as much as a man- *'does not live by bread alone'.* A woman is more than a skivvy for a man; she has equal dignity of mind and spirit with a male, and should be treated with equal consideration. This esteem is reflected in Jesus' words about divorce:

> *'If a husband divorces his wife and marries again, he commits adultery against his wife.' (Luke 16.18)*

Crossan comments:

> *'A man could commit adultery against the rights of another man, but women had no such rights. What Jesus asserts is that women have exactly the same rights as men have in marriage.'*
> *('The Essential Jesus')*

Overall, Jesus puts the relation between male and female on a firm basis of equal respect and mutual affection

US AND THEM

GIVEN the injustices, oppression and cruelties of society, it is inevitable that people developed fear and hatred one of another - and also sometimes contempt: *'Can anything good come from Nazareth?' (John 1.46)* was the reaction of Nathanael to Jesus. Nathanael came from Cana, about 8 miles from Nazareth. If people living in neighbouring villages and towns could hold each other in contempt or as rivals, what must the attitude of more remote folk have been to each other?

'Jews do not share drinking-vessels with Samaritans', John (4.9) informs his readers. Why so? The Samaritans appear to have been a distinct community of Hebrews, perhaps since the 11th century BC. This may account for their religious centre being on Mount Gerizim in Samaria rather than on Mount Zion in Judea, founded by King David around 1000 BC... Also, they esteemed the Five Books of Moses (The Pentateuch) alone as Scripture, contrary to the Jews. Such differences led to the well-documented hostility between Samaritans and Jews.

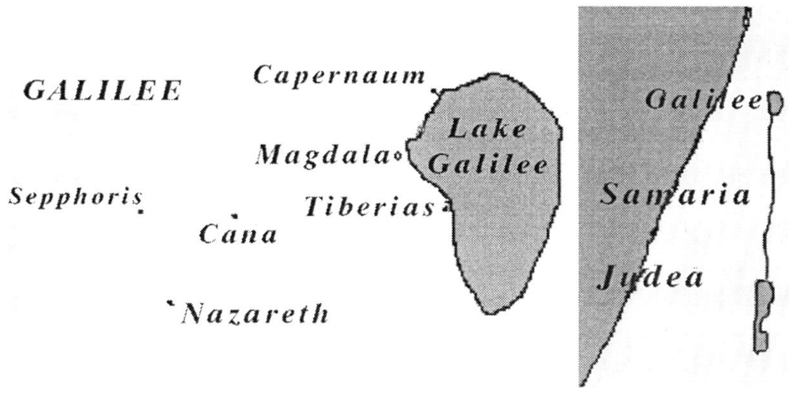

As for the Greeks and Romans in Palestine, as invaders, conquerors, and in various degrees oppressors of the native people, there was 'little love lost' between them.

All this hostility, prejudice and conflict constituted a failure, burden and waste of human life. Jesus, in God's name, sought to transform this. He drew people's attention to the fact, already mentioned, that *'God makes his sun rise on good and bad alike.'* God is not hostile to any people, nor shows spite to those who do wrong. So Jesus calls for a changed, positive attitude to people who oppose us: *'love your enemies and pray for your persecutors' (Matthew 5.44).* He also urged people to put past wrongs behind them by forgiveness - as God forgives *(Matthew 18.23-4).* Further he advises folk not to retaliate; *'an eye for an eye' (Matthew 5.39b-40).* He underscores the importance of trying to put things right with someone aggrieved by regarding reconciliation to have priority over religious observance *(Matthew 5.23-4).* He also makes it crystal-clear that this positive, friendly attitude to people is boundless. This is the point of the parable of the 'good Samaritan' *(Luke 10.30-7).* Jesus is grieved both by the hostility within the nuclear family, as in his parable of the 'father and his two sons' *(Luke 15.11-32)*, and by the enmity between the Jewish nation and their Gentile neighbours as when he approached Jerusalem and *'wept over it'*, saying,

> *'If only you had known this day the way that leads to peace! But no; it is hidden from your sight... ' (Luke 19.42)*

'A Samaritan... was moved to pity'

Jesus' words once again were matched by his deeds. So, when Jesus made such a deep impression on the people of Capernaum that they wished him to stay, he said:

> *'Let us move on to the country towns in the neighbourhood; I have to proclaim my message there also: that is what I came out to do.' Mark then notes; 'So, all through Galilee Jesus went..' (1.38-9).*

Jesus' care for people knew no bounds or frontiers.

Another incident showed Jesus' boundless goodwill and respect. When he was refused entry to a Samaritan village, his disciples called on him to punish them. Jesus refused, saying that he *'did not come to destroy men's lives but to save them'* and went on to another village. *(Luke 9.51-6).*

SUCH was the grand mission of Jesus:
to transform hatred into friendship,
contempt into respect,
and isolationism into comradeship
everywhere on Earth!

POVERTY AND RICHES

We have seen (pp. 55-56) how poverty and hunger existed alongside great wealth. This caused much bitterness and strife, and was largely caused by selfishness and greed. Poverty led to malnutrition and sickness, and this constituted in Jesus' view an affront to God's value of each human being; it was a denial of the caring and sharing society of God's desire the *'kingdom of God'.* Jesus proclaimed:

> *'How blest are you who are in need (Greek-ptochos=destitute); the kingdom of God is yours. How blest are you who now go hungry; your hunger shall be satisfied' (Luke 6.20-1).*

He encouraged people to pray to God: *'Give us today our daily bread'. (Luke11.3).* That is, pray for enough food for each day.

But how will people's prayers be answered? Jesus called on those who had enough and to spare to share with those who had next to nothing. It could well be that Jesus himself first shared his bread as he took part in the movement of John the Baptist. We recall John's practice:

> *'The man who has two shirts must share with him who has none, and anyone who has food must do the same (Luke 3.1).*

Jesus later urged:

> *'When you are having guests for lunch or supper, do not invite your friends, your brothers or other relations, or your rich neighbours; they will only ask you back again and so you will be repaid. But when you give a party, ask the poor, the crippled, the lame and the blind' (Luke 14.12-13).*

Jesus and his disciples put this teaching into practice. They embarked on a mission in which they healed people and, in turn, received their hospitality. Women followers shared by providing sustenance for the disciples out of their own resources. This was the formation of a sharing community. This activity, writes Crossan:

> *'...was not merely a strategy for supporting the mission... (but) for building, or rebuilding, peasant community on... the sharing of spiritual and material power at the most grassroots level.'*

Could it not well be also that behind the 'feeding of the five thousand', treated as a miracle by later interpreters, was the practical sharing of food with one another? We also note Jesus' exhortation to the *'man of great wealth': 'Go, sell everything you have, and give to the poor.' (Mark 10.21)* Zacchaeus too, the rich superintendent of taxes, climbed a tree to listen to Jesus' teaching. The two became friends, and Zacchaeus was inspired to *'give half my possessions to charity'. (Luke 19.8)*

So, Jesus' followers lived as they prayed:

'Father... your kingdom come... give us each day our daily bread.' (Luke 11.3)

They lived in God's kingdom where the rich share daily bread with the poor.

Here we may attend to Jesus' basic attitude to wealth.

'It is easier for a camel to pass through the eye of a needle than for a rich man to enter the kingdom of God.' (Mark 10.25)

Crossan perceptively comments: *'Possessions as such are not considered to be evil... the question is how the rich became rich in the first place.'* 'Tainted' wealth often came through patrons making clients into debtors and dispossessing their land; or public officials using dishonest tricks to increase their income. As long as they impoverish others, they are working against the fairness of God's kingdom. Wealth in any case should be put in the right order of life's priorities.

'Beware, be on your guard against greed of every kind', Jesus said 'for even when a man has more than enough, his wealth does not give him life.'

He proceeded to advise:

'Put away anxious thoughts about food to keep you alive and clothes to cover your body. Life is more than food, the body more than clothes.' (Luke 12. 15,22,23)

As God feeds the birds and clothes the flowers, so he knows that we humans need food and clothing, but our priority must be to seek God's kingdom: that is, to care and share God's material providence fairly with our fellow-citizens. This will end poverty. So the law and 'best practice' of God's kingdom is summarised in the 'golden rule':

'Always treat others as you would like them to treat you.' (Matthew 7.12)

HIGHER AND LOWER ORDERS

THE 'golden rule' implies the tremendous principle of *EQUALITY.* This leads to the most radical and revolutionary practice of Jesus' whole programme for human society. The challenge of Jesus' 'root and branch' way of life is emphasised by J. D. Crossan in *'Jesus, a Revolutionary Biography'.* He quotes the description of the prevailing 1st century society by the historian, David Gilmore:

'(Society) had strong urban orientation, and disdain for the peasant way of life and manual labour.'

Crossan also writes:

'For those who take their very identity from the eyes of their peers, the idea of eating and living together without any distinctions...

discriminations or hierarchies is close to the irrational and the absurd.'

Jesus speaks out against this stratified society. Referring to the doctors of the law and the Pharisees, he says,

> *'They go about with broad phylacteries (black boxes worn on the forehead containing Scripture passages) and with large tassels on their robes; they like to have places of honour at feasts and the chief seats in synagogues; to be greeted respectfully in the street and to be addressed as 'rabbi' (that is, "my great one"; master; teacher).'*

Jesus calls for a reversal:

> *'You must not be called 'rabbi'; for you have one Rabbi, and you are all brothers.' (Matthew 23.5-8)*

The call for equality is made also in the parable of 'The invitation to the banquet'. When those at first invited have excused themselves the host instructs his servant: *'Go out quickly into the streets of the town, and bring in as many people as you can find.'* Crossan comments that the result of such an open invitation could be that guests of different 'classes', 'ranks' and sexes would come and share the same table - and 'of such is the kingdom of God'. *(Luke 14.15-23)* It is in this vein that Jesus says:

> *'Many who are first will be last, and the last first... The mighty will be brought down. The lowly will be raised up.' (Matthew 23.12)*

This revolution in society is further emphasised when Jesus deals with the desire for high places in his movement by two brothers, James and John. He says:

> *'You know that among the Gentiles the recognised rulers lord it over their subjects, and the great make their authority felt. It shall not be so with you; among you, whoever wants to be great must be your servant, and whoever wants to be first must be the slave of all.'*
> *(Mark 10.42-4)*

Jesus practises what he preaches, according to John's Gospel, when he washes his disciples' feet. *(John 13.5)* This action is not just a ritual; it is an instance of Jesus' whole way of life - an end to society's distinctions and hierarchies, the exaltation of manual labour, and the inauguration of the tradition of service to people.

The usual order of society is to have 'too many chiefs', who love to be superior and to be served, and 'not enough Indians', prepared to 'roll up their sleeves', get their hands dirty, and get on with the job.

But in the kingdom of God, Jesus' society, there are no 'chiefs', because *everyone* is an 'Indian'!

HERE ENDS the catalogue of troubles that Jesus aimed to 'shoot'!

"WANTED – MORE TROUBLE-SHOOTERS"

JESUS' 'grand mission' to show God's love, to save each human soul, and transform human society needed *many* workers. *'The harvest is abundant,'* Jesus said, *'but the workers are few; beg therefore the master of the harvest to send out workers into his harvest' (Luke 10.2).* As with many movements, large or small, through history -Buddhism, the Hebrew prophets, the Pharisees- Jesus gathered around him a band of disciples-learners, and took much care in training them for their mammoth and arduous task.

He taught them by example 'on the job'. (See *Mark 9.14-29)* He also practised delegation of responsibility, giving the disciples 'hands-on' experience. *'He sent them out two by two with authority over unclean spirits.'* (See *Mark 6.7-13)* Yet, he did not neglect to help them to relax and 'stand back' to assess their mission with him. (See *Mark 6.31-2)*

Most importantly, if they were to be capable of carrying out this radical mission, Jesus knew that they needed *special and genuine qualifications.*

JOB-DESCRIPTION OF A 'TROUBLE-SHOOTER'

- **First and foremost you will practise what you preach.** The kingdom of God begins in *your* mind and soul; you require God's Spirit of trust and love, helping you to 'lead from the front'. Remember Jesus' saying: *'What if those who are the salt must themselves be seasoned?'* - 'Handsome is as handsome does'!

- **You will not hoard the truths you learned, but share them.** Remember: *'What I tell you in the dark, speak in the light. And what you hear as a whisper, proclaim on the housetops.' (Matthew 10.27)*

- **You will not 'blindly' follow anyone - or public opinion- but seek the truth.** Only when truth is personally discovered can one confidently go forward or guide others. *'The blind lead the blind right into the ditch.' (Matthew 15.14)*

- **You will be ready to cooperate with anyone who is not against God's kingdom.** *'Those who are not against you are for you.' (Mark 9.40)* (See this in action, *Mark 9.39*)

- **You will be in a small pioneer movement, but like a little leaven in a lump of dough you can achieve much.** Remember the parable in *Matthew 13.33.*

- **You will accept that the Gospel will often fall on deaf ears.** Yet your persistence will uncover other ready hearers. Look up the parable in *Matthew 13.3-8.*

- **You will be prepared for the 'long haul' of caring for people.** Remember the protracted responsibility of parenthood - and *'a builder planning a tower* *first counts the cost. A ruler planning a campaign first counts the army.' (Luke 14.28-32)*

- **You will be wise to guileful people, but will not repay with dirty tricks.** *'Be guileful as snakes. Be guileless as doves.' (*Matthew *10.16)*
- **When you challenge bad behaviour, you will be prepared to be badly treated.** *'We walk in the shadow of the cross.' (Matthew 10.38)*

THE TROUBLE-SHOOTER IS SHOT – FATALLY

THE last qualification for a Trouble-Shooter, as listed, proved to be grievously applicable to the 'recruiter'! It was all too inevitable that he who challenged ingrained bad behaviour should himself be badly treated. It seems that Jesus' actions in the Temple in Jerusalem at Passover-time, according to many New Testament scholars, made up the immediate confrontation that led to his arrest and crucifixion.

There were bundled together in the Temple so many abuses of personal and collective life and religion against which Jesus had campaigned. He had a great respect for and affinity with the Hebrew prophets who themselves had been outspoken about basically the same wrongs:

> *'Your countless sacrifices, what are they to me? says the Lord.*
> *I am sated with whole offerings of rams..*
> *Wash and be clean; put away your evil deeds far from my sight;*
> *cease to do evil, learn to do good.'*
> *(Isaiah 1.11,16)*
> *'Am I to come before God with whole-offerings, with yearling calves?..*
> *what is it that the Lord requires of you; only to act justly,*
> *to love loyalty, to walk humbly with your God.'*
> *(Micah 6.7,8)*

Jesus found the Temple's 'Court of the Gentiles' particularly crowded with the marketing of sacrifices. *Mark* tells of *'dealers in pigeons'* and *'the tables of the moneychangers' (Mark 11.15).* ('Secular' coins had to be exchanged for 'Sacred' currency.) This Court, meant to be a *'house of prayer' for all nations' (Mark 11.17),* had been taken over by an area of commerce. J. W. Bowman writes in 'The Life and Teaching of Jesus' (Peake's Commentary):

> *'It was mere mockery to suppose that genuine worship could be conducted in the midst of the obvious confusion of a marketplace.'*

This was for Jesus a misappropriation of God's house. Yet more, the relation between God and humankind, as the prophets had argued, is spiritual and moral, and broken relations are mended by confession, forgiveness and amendment of life, not by animal sacrifices. Right human relationships are not transactions made with the 'coinage' of sacrifice, nor by employing a 'broker' such as a priest. The Temple however as Jesus saw it was the epitome of a

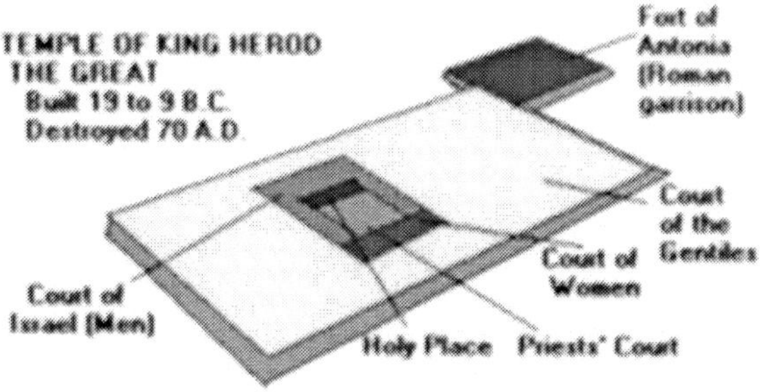

venue for barter and brokerage.

Another item in the bundle of abuses connected with the commerce was the temptation to greed and the amassing of great wealth and power. Lawrence H. Schiffman writes in an article on 'Priests' in 'Harper's Bible Dictionary':

> *'The Roman procurators appointed the high priests (of the Temple) many of whom bought the office through their great wealth. These families created an oligarchy of power and prestige, and were regarded by the Pharisees as tyrannical to the peasants and sympathisers with the Romans.'*

This situation offended Jesus' belief in the equality of people before God, and the uplifting of the poor from their destitution.

The Temple also was the embodiment of social division and discrimination, sexually, internationally and religiously. The various Courts separated Gentiles from Jews, men from women, priests from laity, and priestly rank from rank. The unhappy divisions of daily life were merely underlined by the Temple. This denied the universal love of *'neighbour'* that Jesus had lived to promote.

So, there was no place within 'striking-distance' of Jesus where all the troubles of society were focused to compare with the Jerusalem Temple. Here then was the site to demonstrate his radical and positive remedy for those ills. The German New Testament scholar, Herder, made a connection with the previous event of the feeding of 5000 people. These people according to *John's Gospel (6.15) 'meant to proclaim him king'*. Jesus refused, because, according to Herder, he wanted to make his move at a time and place where it would have a maximum influence on people's lives. That time and place was at the Passover Festival when Jerusalem was crowded with pilgrims from countries far and wide, and converging on the Temple.

So, Ben F. Meyer writes in 'The Aims of Jesus':

'Planned for "prime-time" and maximum exposure, this demonstration was calculated to interrupt business as usual and bring the presence of God's reign abruptly and forcefully to the attention of all... it was also a fulfillment event and sign of the future.'

Jesus' action was symbolic: it was not an insurrection. It was in modern terms a 'demonstration', containing a message like the acts of the Hebrew prophets. The acted message was that the freely-given love and forgiveness of God is available for *all* people without distinction. It was not an armed rebellion, because killing was not Jesus' way. Furthermore, he and his relatively few followers had no military chance against the might of the Roman garrison in the Antonia Tower overlooking the Temple.

However, Jesus' deeds quickly brought reaction from the priestly authorities and their Roman allies. Jesus was arrested, condemned and crucified by the imperial authority, probably as being a dangerous prophet, an 'unruly element', and by way of a deterrent to others.

'They brought Jesus to the place called Golgotha, which means 'Place of a Skull'... It was nine in the morning when they crucified him.' (Mark 15.22,25)

JESUS LIVES ON

THE CRUCIFIXION OF JESUS would have caused shock and gloom in his followers. *'The flame is quenched... the stream is run into the sand!'*

Some such metaphors would describe the feelings of some at least of his disciples. Jesus and his mission which had raised in them such faith, hope and love had, to use another figure, *'run into the buffers'.* IT WAS ALL OVER!

BUT THAT WAS JUST NOT SO! Contrary verdicts about the Christian belief in the Resurrection of Jesus are arrived at by non-Christian historians of the period as well as by Christian scholars, whether of a fundamentalist or liberal inclination.

WHAT happened to Jesus after his death?

- Was his body revived, to walk out of the tomb?
- Did Jesus' followers receive an 'apparition' of him?
- Did the disciples become convinced that Jesus was still with them 'in spirit', empowering them – and with God in heaven?

Close study of the New Testament gives no certain favour to any of these alternatives. Whilst the Gospels tell of the empty tomb, several of the instances recounted in them of meetings between Jesus and his disciples after his death fit in with the belief that the encounter was an apparition, not a sight of a

> ***WHAT happened to Jesus after his death***
> - *Was his body revived, to walk out of the tomb?*
> - *Did Jesus' followers receive an apparition of him?*
> - *Did the disciples become convinced that Jesus was still with them 'in spirit', empowering them - and with God in heaven?*

physical body. (Read Luke 24.15,16,31 and John 20.19*)*. This verdict has support from the testimony of the apostle Paul. He writes to the Christians in Galatia:

> *'God... chose to reveal his son in and through me, in order that I might proclaim him among the Gentiles.' (Letter to the Galatians 1.15,16).*

Paul classes this revelation/apparition to him - not a meeting with Jesus in the flesh - with the appearances of the risen Jesus to Cephas (Peter), the Twelve (apostles), and to James, Jesus' brother.

Yet, however inconsistent are the accounts and beliefs, the fact of the continuation of a relationship between Jesus and his followers is indisputable!

This is most tellingly substantiated by contemporary Jewish and Roman non-Christian historians.

Josephus wrote 60 years after Jesus' crucifixion:

> *'... (when he was crucified) those who had in the first place come to love him did not give up their affection for him... and the tribe of Christians, so called after him, has still to this day not disappeared.'*

Tacitus, the Roman, recorded in the early 2nd century:

> *'The pernicious superstition (Christianity) was checked for the moment, only to break our once more.'*

The 20th century student of Jesus and Judaism, E. P. Sanders, also concludes a meticulous survey of the Christian proclamation of the 'resurrection' by asking us to consider this: how could the immediate followers of Jesus have risked ridicule and even threats to their lives by championing the condemned and crucified one, and telling publicly that Jesus had been raised to new life, if nothing of significance had happened to make them believe that he who had died now lived on?

J. D. Crossan believes that the initial and significant experience of these first followers was their conviction that after his death Jesus was still with them 'in spirit'. Crossan expands on this in 'Jesus, a Revolutionary Biography':

> *'Did they all stop their activities on the day of his death? Did they all immediately lose their faith? Or, if they found themselves just as empowered as before, was he not somehow still with them - and how could that presence best be expressed?'*

'A PRESENT HELP IS HE'

WE can, of course, today neither prove nor disprove Jesus' resurrection, and it is clearly wrong to castigate, as some do, anyone for having doubts about it.

Nevertheless, what in the end is important is that just as the earliest disciples continued their relationship of faith, hope and love with Jesus after his death, and were in Crossan's word *'empowered'* to labour in proclaiming God's kingdom, so in all the succeeding centuries Jesus' followers have lived with him 'in spirit', and served God in the power of the same Spirit - as *we* can right now!

The words of countless Christians, especially writers of hymns, express this faith and experience of all of us who try to follow Jesus today. So, the 19th century English headmaster, Henry Twells, wrote of Jesus:

'Thy touch has still its ancient power;
no word from Thee can fruitless fall... '

And the American, Ray Palmer, sang:

'I see Thee not, I hear Thee not,
yet art Thou oft with me... '

But finally we come to a contemporary author, Brian Wren, who puts our comradeship with the still-living Jesus 'in a nutshell':

'There's a spirit in the air,
telling Christians everywhere:
Praise the love that Christ revealed,
living, working, in our world.'

MAKING SENSE OF LIFE - BOOK THREE

GOD AND THE MORAL WORLD

Part One

Basic Principles

GOD LOVES US

Body & Soul

and ALL of us together

'GOD AND THE MORAL WORLD'

I don't know, Dear Reader, what your reaction is to this phrase-title. Maybe you will consider that both 'God' and a 'Moral World' are fictions, abstractions, fancies. If you have just lived through a devastating earthquake or the horror of a massacre, you can be forgiven for your cynicism and rejection of the very notion of 'GOD' or of a 'MORAL WORLD'!

However, the thrust of what you are about to read is the conviction that both God and the Moral World are far from fiction: on the contrary we try to show how real and solid they are, and how vital they are to the success and happiness of all our lives. Indeed we search in *Part 1* of this Book for the *BASIC PRINCIPLES* of a moral life in God's world and begin with a real-life incident.

JIMMY BOYLE, a young Glaswegian, was convicted of murder. His life-imprisonment in a 'house of correction' was proving disastrous. 'Correction' was far from the reality. Jimmy reacted to his 'custodial sentence' extremely violently: so much so that he was passed from one prison to another, always lashing out at warders and often only restrained by manacles and padded-cells. His life and soul were chaotic and he bade to wreak havoc wherever he went.

Yet after a time even he grew weary of his behaviour. The moral turning-point came when one day a warder slipped a bar of chocolate into his cell. Jimmy realised that in spite of all the mayhem he had caused someone thought he was worth caring for; that in the midst of the immoral chaos there was another world, a better, caring, ordered life – a *moral* world; and that he was being invited into it. Moreover he himself could change into a better, caring, ordered, *moral* person.

He did just that. Step by step he gathered his life together, learned how to respect and care for other people, and began a new career of service to folk in trouble as he had been.

LIKE A MOTOR CAR

JIMMY BOYLE'S experience illustrates several features involved in living in the *moral world.*

We may compare these features with those of a MOTOR CAR.

1st DIMENSION	Car Body = *Human Body & Physical World*
2nd DIMENSION	Passenger-seating = *Relations with Other People*
3rd DIMENSION	(Hidden) Chassis = *My (unseen) Human Soul*

All three *dimensions* of our *moral* life, *soul, body and relations,* are 'powered' by the LOVE OF GOD!

GOD AND THE MORAL WORLD - UNITY AND COMPLEXITY

UNITY. As the frame of a motor car and its engine are dependent on each other, so are the dimensions of the *moral world.* My body and the physical world around me, other people and my soul are intimately related to each other and to the Personal God, who made them all. God links each dimension into a unity, and the appreciation of this unity must infuse all our moral thought and action.

COMPLEXITY. Within the unity is complexity. It is vital that we pay attention to the *variety* of *parts* of any phenomenon or situation, whether a flower, an aeroplane, or a football-team; whether a choice of several courses of action, or forming a partnership, or sorting out a quarrel. How crucial for example in even as simple a chore as cooking porridge, that its temperature, ingredients and seasoning all be carefully considered! Neglect of any one item could spell disaster! Just so with our *moral* concerns: each detail requires special treatment. Let us begin with concerns *within my soul.*

THE MORAL WORLD - THE FIRST DIMENSION - WITHIN MY SOUL

> *'Two things fill me with awe', said the philosopher, Immanuel Kant, 'the starry heavens above, and the MORAL LAW WITHIN'.*

The author of the Hebrew Psalm 51 was conscious of the wrong within his soul: *'For well I know my misdeeds, and my sins confront me all day long.'*

When I choose between good and bad, right and wrong, that is *morality.* This implies that the *moral world* resides *within my soul*, wherever else it may exist.

Modern psychology has sought to describe the activity of the soul. (See also *Book One, Part 2, pp.22-23)* Sigmund Freud suggested that the soul partakes in the *unity* and *complexity* of all phenomena, as shown in the illustration.

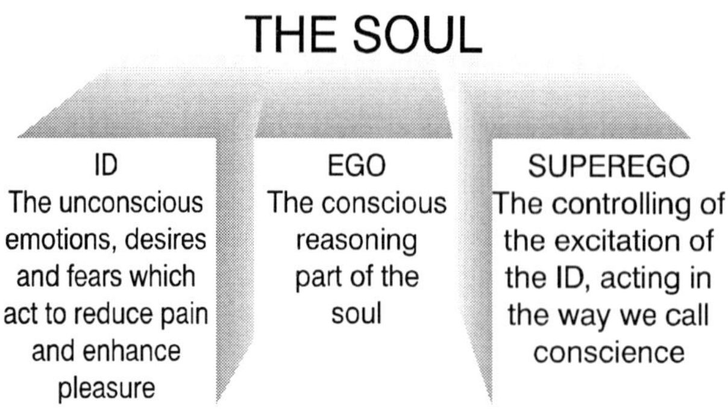

This inner activity of the soul, however, is affected from outside. Students of moral development like H. Hartstone and M. A. May in the USA traced that progress whereby the amoral infant, who is an active learner, acquires his or her first moral standards from the parents. The child watches the parents and copies their actions and speech, and seeks to avoid their displeasure and punishment. Soon teachers and friends have a similar influence on the inner conscience and moral actions of the growing person.

We copy and are influenced by other people, but at the same time our own soul develops its ID, EGO and SUPEREGO (desire, reason and conscience).

So, we move on from being an imitator of other people's moral behaviour towards being an originator of moral conduct; from being an irresponsible person to being a responsible one. The 'baton' of choice is handed over to us.

One choice follows another:

- should I smoke cigarettes?
- should I buy that expensive dress?
- should I observe the speed-limit?
- should I keep to a diet?
- should I tell a lie to gain an advantage over someone?

How does this process of choice work? We take the example of 'to smoke or not to smoke cigarettes? 'I may feel the *desire* to smoke, yet my *reason* may inform me that my health will suffer thereby. Then my *conscience* will tell me that it is morally wrong to defy my reason. *My whole soul must decide!'*

The key operator in this process of choice is my *conscience*. It is one of the most high-powered of human abilities. It acts like a set of traffic-lights: telling me to go for what is good; to pause in what is doubtful; and to stop doing what is bad. It enables me to succeed in life's enterprises, and to avoid disastrous activities. However, like a highly-charged machine, the conscience can do harm in certain circumstances by producing excessive feelings of guilt, and inhibiting innocent, wholesome activity. Conscience needs careful handling. This is done if we keep aware of its positive purpose as well as its negative power.

Furthermore, each choice I make in itself may or may not have far-reaching consequences. Each one is the 'little drop of water that makes a mighty ocean'. Each choice has a cumulative effect, increasing -or diminishing- the quality of my moral life. Each decision either strengthens or weakens my ability to choose the right. This process within my soul is vital to my soul's well-being - and to my body's health, and my relation to other souls.

Finally, however strong my soul may be, I remain vulnerable. The outcome of my conscience's contention with my own desires or those of other people is not a foregone conclusion. My desires or the coercion of others can be extremely powerful. My soul is continually 'under siege'. But maybe, as with the British army at Mafeking, there is relief from outside by way of a victorious force? Does such a force exist?

ALL YOU NEED IS LOVE - GOD'S LOVE

YES, there is an 'outside force'. Recall the action that changed Jimmy Boyle's life. The gift to him of a bar of chocolate was the outward and visible sign of the inward, invisible intention -the love- of the prison warder, even though he may not have described what he did as 'love'. Another's love brought relief.

What is *LOVE?* Like a *cake* it is composed of several ingredients

- *AFFECTION (*delight in & affection for someone)
- *RESPECT* (treating someone as you would like to be treated)
- *HUMILITY* (admission of faults)
- *DETERMINATION* (steely persistence in love*)*

Jimmy Boyle received love from his warder. Where did the warder's love come from? *LOVE originates in the PERSONAL GOD.* (Book One, Part 2)

So, a beloved and respected Sunday School Teacher in Oldham, Elaine Everett, testified, *'I am loved'.* She meant 'loved by God'. Such is the *'white-heat of the love of God'* shown by Jesus. *(Book Two, Part 1)*

My soul, my conscience, learns of this powerful 'ally', GOD, and when my soul accepts God's love I am given God's affection and respect for me; the humility to confess my faults; and the determination to keep on loving through all opposition and weariness.

The significance of accepting God's love is explained in an excerpt from the film, *'The Earthling'.* An ageing man is going home to die in his native Australia. He shares his life's wisdom with a recently-orphaned boy. He says:

'Never be afraid of love; and always show it!'

Why might I 'be afraid of love'? I may feel unworthy: my thoughts and deeds don't deserve love. Perhaps I don't want to risk being let down. But the love of God experienced by some Biblical authors and proclaimed by Jesus (Book *Two, Part 1)* is offered to my undeserving and fearful soul. This is a genuine love as defined above: affectionate, respectful, humble and determined; a *'love that never ends' (1 Corinthians 13.8)*

'And always show it.' A retired headteacher in Preston summed up effective teaching by asserting:

'No impression without expression.'

Equally love's growth is arrested if it is not shown to others: love strengthens the more it is practised.

HERE then, we find the BASIC PRINCIPLE of *'GOD AND THE MORAL WORLD'.*

GOD has the supreme influence on my soul.
God is my soul's Lover and Saviour, as Jesus showed.
I receive into my soul God's affection, respect. humility and determination.
God allies himself with me to contend with wrong,
and strengthens me to choose the right.
My (moral) strength is as the strength of ten,
because God is with my soul. *

* *Apologies to Tennyson*

THE supremacy of God's love in the moral world within my soul as well as in my relations with the physical world and other souls - has implications for other wide- spread and influential human beliefs, which are really *incompatible* with God's supremacy, and are injurious to the soul's morality - as we shall now show.

BELIEF IN THE DEVIL AND HELL HAVE 'PASSED THEIR SELL-BY DATE'

THE DEVIL

THE first belief that is incompatible with GOD as SUPREMELY LOVE is the notion of a *spiritual-supernatural power opposing God.* Various names have been given for this 'power': *'The Devil', 'Satan', 'The Antichrist'* in Jewish and Christian parlance, or *'Angra Mainyu' (evil spirit)* in the Parsi religion, as an example from eastern faiths.

Should however a Christian Minister declare that he or she doesn't believe in the devil - nor in Hell - there arises immediately from some Christians a certain amount of consternation!

Dismay soon turns to argument.

'If you say there is no Devil, how can you say there is God?' If you deny Hell, is there no Heaven either?'

It seems to many believers that the power of good (God) and evil (Devil) are all 'part of the furniture', or as essential pieces of a complete 'jigsaw' of the *moral world.* What justification can there be to break up the 'set'?

Justification rests upon the nature and moral character of God. (Book *One, Part 2 & Book Two, Part 1*)

GOD is the sole origin of the universe (all that exists). God is also consistently good and loving. It follows that the existence of a Devil, a spiritual, supernatural power opposing God, would be against that consistency, and unjustifiable, because it would imply that the good God had deliberately created an evil superpower, the Devil. That is absurd.

Yet, the question still arises: *'Are you denying that EVIL exists?'* No. Evidence of evil appears in every murder, theft, act of adultery or rape, in every pogrom and massacre. This is an absolute fact. but we are asking; *'Where does evil come from? What is the nature of this evil power?'*

EVIL - man's inhumanity to man

Someone who believes in the existence of the devil appears to answer these questions by arguing that evil is a supernatural power on a par with the power of goodness, God. If there is God, the being and source of good, then there has to be the Devil, the being and source of evil. This argument is not logical: for this reason - *God,* the Creator of all and the Author of all goodness *exists* (that is the belief of this author Book *One, Part 2*), but is there an *Anti-God* or an *Anti-Author* of all badness? That does not follow (see right).

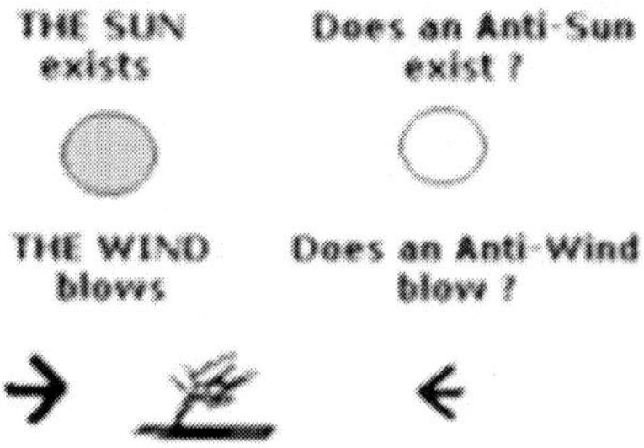

GOD
is the only supernatural being
and is consistently good

Rather, the 'bottom line' is:

No Anti-God!

Where then does evil come from, and what is its nature?

EVIL is... *when one man strikes another; when one slanders another... Such actions are manifestations of selfishness or jealousy or hatred;* that is 'evil'.

EVIL comes from... *human faults. Sayings from two of the foremost English poets lead straight to the real and* only *origin of 'evil'.*

Shakespeare's Cassius in *'Julius Caesar'* says:

> *'The fault, dear Brutus, is not in our stars, but in ourselves, that we are underlings.'*

Milton's *'Satan'*(!) ejected from heaven, waxes defiant, but tells the truth about good and evil, peace or turmoil of mind:

> *'The mind is in its own place, and in itself*
> *Can make a Heav'n of Hell, a Hell of Heav'n.'*

Evil is not 'out there'. It is not some warped, divine power, nor an evil-fate. Evil is not supernatural *'principalities... powers... spiritual wickedness in high places' (Ephesians 6.12 AV).* Evil does not enter my soul from outside the human realm: although as with goodness and love evil may be transmitted from one soul to another. Rather, evil grows in our own mind and soul through our own superstition, fear and selfishness. It then breaks out in all the faults listed by the apostle Paul: *'fornication, indecency, debauchery, quarrels, a contentious temper, envy, fits of rage, selfish ambitions...' (Galatians 5.19,20).*

We can support this view of the origin of evil with evidence from three aspects of our human experience.

- The world of our primitive ancestors was filled with natural powers many of which made them afraid: perishing cold and searing heat; hurricane, flood and earthquake; fire and pestilence; awesome wild animals and hostile fellow-humans. Little wonder then that they developed terror, aggressive feelings and fierce warlike traits. The last is revealed for example 3000 years ago by the people of Cerro Sechin in present-day Peru, who inflicted grotesque cruelties on their enemies. (Cited in Richard Leakey's *'The Making of Mankind', p.219)* It is relevant to note, then, that from *human* fear, selfishness and aggression came the belief in *superhuman* powers of evil and ill-will. Men gave them various names such as *Yamm* (Prince Sea and Ocean Current chaos) or *Mot* (God of death and sterility). *Shiva,* one of the three principal Hindu deities, can be both creative and destructive like nature. He is often depicted holding weapons, or with a third eye capable of destroying whoever it looks out on. So, the evil-devil arose from human fear of the perils of life.
- Still in today's world 'primitive' superstitious beliefs are found. In South Africa's Northern Province a woman was struck by lightning. Villagers summoned witch doctors to identify a fellow-villager, believed to be possessed by an evil-spirit and responsible for the stricken victim's injury. Eventually a Mr. Mpai was pointed out and condemned to death by stoning. The real culprit, lightning, was substituted by an 'evil spirit'

- When we are little children, near the beginning of our conscious life, we do not differentiate between fact and imagination: between a Christmas gift and 'Father Christmas' who delivers it; between a factual malevolent person and a 'witch'; between a real temptation and a belief in 'Satan' as a 'tempter'. Only experience and thought start to separate reality from fiction

These reflections show that the *'Devil* is the mistaken and often fearful invention of our mind rather than a reality 'out there'. Truly, the 'Devil' has passed his *'sell-by date'*! And because of the results of this belief, not before time! For what havoc has followed! As disastrous as the dropping of a cluster-bomb is the spread of belief in the 'Devil'. The fear, selfishness and aggression in the human soul is magnified by the dimension of devil-belief; human faults are exaggerated into gross iniquities; malevolent persons become 'witches'; mentally-deranged souls are deemed to be 'demon-possessed' and a powerful nation becomes the 'great Satan'. Once 'demonised' a 'devil-possessed' person can, it is claimed, be rightly persecuted, even tortured. This is a tragic progression. For sure, the human soul can be *'desperately wicked' (Jeremiah 17.9)*. This however is no warrant to add another dimension to our sin: the supernatural 'Devil'. No!

The sole reality of evil is the sin of the human soul.

It is *my* sin that must be dealt with; not the inflated fantasy of the 'Devil'. Frances Hill shows this in *'A Delusion of Satan: the Full Story of the Salem Witch Trials'.* The Salem Puritans tended to place wicked behaviour outside of their group into 'enemy' souls - 'witches' - of whom they executed seventeen!

EVIL IS NO MATCH FOR GOD

I need to find the right balance in *the moral world within my soul.* The *evil in my soul* (not in any 'Devil') is set against the *goodness and mercy of God.* These are the two realities. The evil in my soul is strong, but is no match for the goodness of God! This is stated vividly by George Fox, founder of the Quakers:

> *'I looked on the world, and saw an ocean of darkness;*
> *but over and above I saw a greater ocean of light.'*

The Hebrew seer who inspired his people to recover from defeat by the Babylonians in the 6th century BC realised the overwhelming power of God's goodness and mercy. He wrote:

> *'To whom will you liken me, whom set up as my equal? says God... The eternal God, creator... does not weary or grow faint... He gives vigour to the weary, new strength to the exhausted...'*
> *(Isaiah 40.25,28-9)*

So is the evil in my soul 'cut down to size'. It cannot finally prevail against the combined power of my conscience and my Maker!

HELL

WE have argued that belief in the 'Devil' is the fantasy of our imagination. Connected to this belief is that of *'HELL'*. How are the two related? The notorious massacre at Dunblane in 1996 suggests the answer.

Thomas Hamilton, the mass-murderer, *could* be thought to have been 'possessed' by an evil spirit, the 'Devil'. Several people who witnessed the carnage certainly described it as 'hell'. So, 'Devil' represents the *doing* or agency of evil, and 'Hell' the *situation* which results. However, more particularly 'Hell' is seen as the situation after human death, it being linked with *Hel*, the Norse guardian of the underworld and of the dead.

We can separate two aspects of the notion of 'Hell'

THE PAIN & DESTRUCTION OF 'HELL'

THE sight of the broken bodies of the children of Dunblane was one reason for calling the situation 'Hell'. Similarly as a convoy of Krajina Serbs fled from Croats they passed through the town of Sisak and were pelted with stones. Danica Trpcevic, her left cheek scarred by a stone, exclaimed, *'We went through 'hell'!'* 'Hell' with its pain and destruction was known to the Jews as *'Gehenna'*, derived from the valley of Hinnom at the foot of Mount Zion, where human sacrifice took place in the 7th century BC., and where later refuse was tipped and corpses of criminals were burned or allowed to decompose. The pain and destruction of the site became a metaphor for 'Hell', God's place of eternal punishment; unquenchable fire. *(Isaiah 66.24)*

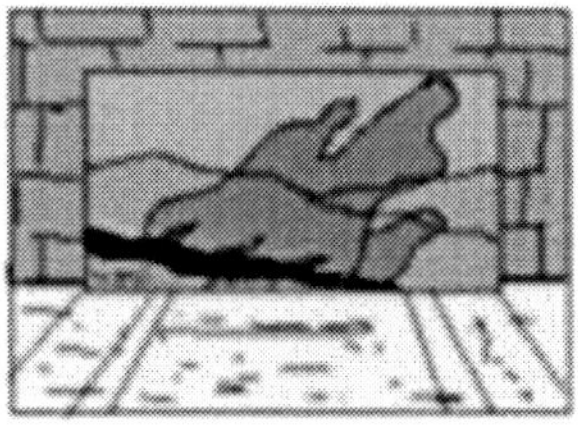

Ancient Jerusalem's Potsherd Gate, leading to the Hinnom Valley (Gehenna), the town's refuse dump.

We see then, how just as the 'Devil' is an inflated human fantasy of evil, 'Hell' is a blown-up fiction of how people inflict pain and slaughter on their fellows. So, a 15th Century French woodcut (right) portrays 'Hell' as on the one hand exceedingly cold, where victims are plunged into an unbearably icy river blown over by a biting wind, and on the other hand as superlatively hot as in turn the damned are thrown into a lake of fire. Such sadistic fantasies are but mild samples of many more cruel and gruesome descriptions of the pain and destruction of 'Hell'

12. THE TORMENT OF COLD.

'HELL' AS CONDEMNATION AND SEPARATION FROM GOD

THE natural human reaction to the cold-blooded murder of the Dunblane children was the unreserved belief that Thomas Hamilton must go to 'Hell', being unfit ever to be with his victims and with God in heaven. Such condemnation and separation from God is the second aspect of the notion of 'Hell'. The condemned sinner will *never be with God!*.

BUT DOES SUCH A 'HELL' REALLY EXIST?

WE have of course no 'firsthand' evidence to prove 'Hell's' existence! Moreover, the faith-testimony in the Bible is, as on many other subjects, contradictory.

- After death we are in *'the land of oblivion' (Psalm 88)*

- *'In God's right hand are pleasures for evermore.' (Psalm 16.11)*
- *'Many of those who sleep in the dust of the earth will awake, some to everlasting life and some to the reproach of eternal abhorrence.' (Daniel 12.2)*
- *'It is better for you to enter into life maimed than to keep both hands and go to hell, to the unquenchable fire.' (Mark 9.43)*

The last quotation is attributed to Jesus, but study of the Gospels *(Book Two, Part 1)* suggests that the original teaching of Jesus has sometimes been overlaid by the views and actions of his followers. There are reasons to show that this is the case here.

How can we square inflicting pain on sinful people or destroying them with the conduct of Jesus as shown in the Gospels as a whole.

- Jesus said, *'It is not the healthy who need a doctor, but the sick. I did not come to call the virtuous, but sinners.' (Mark 2.17)*
- His befriending of imperfect people was so marked that he was accused of being a *'friend of tax-collectors and sinners'. (Luke 7.34)*
- Jesus' care for those regarded as being 'demon-possessed' also shows the opposite of delight in inflicting pain or seeking to punish bad people.
- He also refused to sanction the judicial stoning to death of the woman caught in the act of adultery. *(John 8.1-11)*
- Jesus objected to his disciples' demand for fire to be called down from heaven upon the Samaritans who denied him passage through their village. *(Luke 9.55)*
- (See also *Matthew 5.43-5 & 18.21)*

JESUS, the 'friend of sinners'

We have then in the Gospels diametrically opposed positions on the treatment of wrongdoers or opponents: so much so that we have to choose one position or the other: either the *torture and destruction of sinners in 'Hell'; or their sparing eternally.*

DOES 'HELL' REALLY EXIST? The teaching *and* practice of Jesus, as well as our experience of God's mercy, must decide the answer, and leave us with the faith that, after rebuke, God will forgive and persevere with us in this life and beyond until the moment of confession and abiding reconciliation between each of our souls and God. Such is the faith of the author of *Psalm 130 (vv. 3,4,7)* :

> *'If you, O God, should keep account of sins, who could hold his ground?*
> *But with you is forgiveness, so that you may be revered.'*
> *... For in God is love unfailing, and great is his power to deliver.'*

THE CONSEQUENCES OF BELIEF IN 'HELL'

OUR debate about 'Hell' is far more than a 'talking-point'. It penetrates to the heart of our faith and life. *'What kind of God,* we may well ask:

> *'... would be content to banish a human being to everlasting punishment in 'Hell'?' 'And what quality of morals would be mine if I were to justify human hatred, vengeance and barbaric cruelty by imitating God's (supposed) treatment of the damned?'*

THE SADISTIC CIRCLE

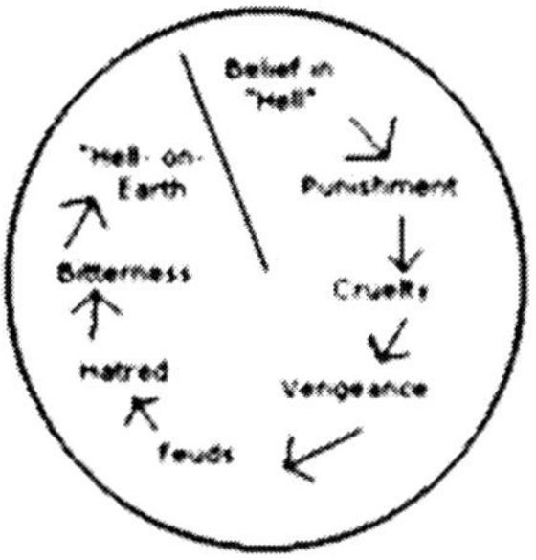

To believe that God condemns someone to everlasting 'hell' creates a *'sadistic circle',* of which we record this example.

> *Sadistic, cruel actions have marked the notorious Mafia. John Follain, writing about the Sicilian Mafia's initiation ritual, describes how the 'boss imitates the local Roman Catholic priest in threatening dire punishments if commandments are violated'. (A Dishonoured Society', p. 34). When a Mafia boss 'makes an offer you can't refuse', perhaps he has in mind the notion that God does the same, when God threatens people with 'Hell-fire'!*

So, Augustine of Hippo, who advocated the doctrine of 'Hell', was the first Christian theologian to urge the employment of force against heretics and schismatics. (See further in Canon Percy Dearmer's 'The Legend of Hell', p.67).

THE GRACIOUS CIRCLE

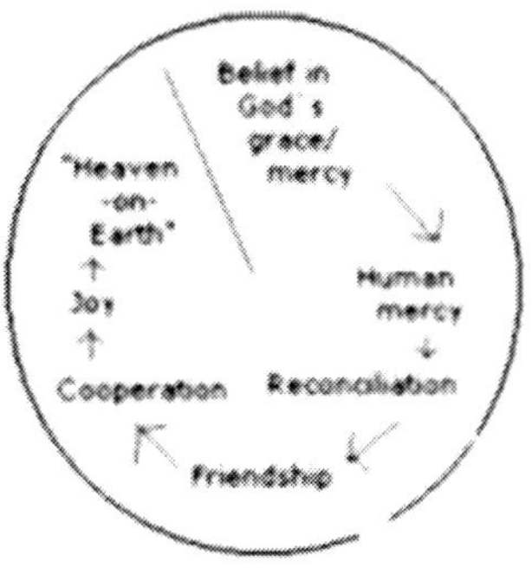

This is the *'sadistic circle'* we wrap around ourselves when we believe that God consigns his 'enemies' (whom Jesus asks us to love!) to 'Hell'.

We contrast this with the *'merciful circle',* when we believe in the eternal forgiveness of God upon us. Then, we can only look with mercy on the worst human being - like Thomas Hamilton - and give him or her time to amend life for ever!

POSTSCRIPT

IF you, Dear Reader, are still convinced that 'Scripture' confirms the existence of 'Hell' as condemnation and separation from God, please consider the text of *1 Corinthians 13.4-8:*

> *'Love is patient and kind... Love will never come to an end.'*

'MY GRACE IS ALL YOU NEED'

THE basic principle of living with God in the moral world *within my soul* is that I LIVE WITH GOD *ALONE.* There is no other *spiritual, supernatural* power beyond my soul to influence me. Further, God is gracious: God wants to save me from my sin. So, the apostle, Paul writes, *'My grace is all you need.' 2 Corinthians 12.9) 'There are spiritual resources (from God)',* writes James Reid commenting on this text, *'that can enable a man to triumph over his defect (sin).'* Above all I receive the *grace* -the favour and mercy of God- unmerited by me, but gladly and freely given by my generous Creator. I have thereby experience of what Don Cupitt in *'Taking Leave of God'* calls *'disinterested love',* that is love shared without desire for any 'pay-back'. Such is the key to Christian morality.

GOD'S disinterested love empowers me to show the same in every aspect of my life. Isn't this the meaning of Ignatius of Loyola's prayer?

> *Teach us, good Lord... to give and not to count the cost..*
> *to labour and not to ask for any reward, save that of knowing that we do your will.'*

THE MORAL WORLD - THE SECOND DIMENSION - THE PHYSICAL WORLD

> *'BODY am I entirely, and nothing else; and "soul" is only a word for something about the body.'*

So wrote Nietzshe in 'Thus Spake Zarathustra'. The whole viewpoint of this book disagrees with Nietzshe's rating of the *soul.* Yet the quotation serves to point out the rating of the *body*. Just as a *pair of compasses* has two essential parts - a fixed point and a movable pencil, so God's creation has two essential parts - the body and the soul. The life God has given to us comprises the interaction of body and soul, the physical and the spiritual world.

Both body and soul are precious to their Maker, and our question now is:

> *'What is the place of morality in the interaction of the physical and spiritual aspects of life?'*

OUR BITTER-SWEET LIFE

WHO among us can be unaware of *'the heartache and the thousand natural shocks that flesh is heir to'* that Shakespeare wrote about? Life in our physical body is not 'an easy ride'!

Neither you nor I wanted to be born, either into a body or as a soul. This seemed to be the case with our grandson on the day he 'came into this world'. His face had a pronounced frown upon it! *'Mother, what have you let me in for?'* seemed to be his attitude! Did he have some prior knowledge of Shakespeare's warning about the *'slings and arrows of outrageous fortune'?* Probably not! Nor could he have imagined his future joy and hilarity as he would savour - aged 11- the comedy of *'Dad's army'*!

WHAT DID *YOU* THINK WAS IN THE WORLD, THE DAY WHEN YOU WERE BORN?

WHAT would you find in your house... your countryside? What would people be like? What would they be doing?

'BEDS OF PAIN' AND 'VALE OF TEARS'

LET'S begin with the *bitter* half of life One of the most explicit and vivid accounts of human suffering was written by the author of *'Job'*:

> *'My body is infested with worms, and scabs cover my skin; it is cracked and discharging, My days pass more swiftly than a weaver's shuttle and come to an end as the thread of life runs out.' (Job 7.5,6)*

Job's ordeal made him bitter:

> *'Perish the day when I was born, and the night which said, "A boy is conceived."... why was I not concealed like an untimely birth, like an infant who never saw the light?' (3.3,16)*

Bodily life for Job was distasteful, to say the least. His body was his enemy and so was his Creator, God:

> *'The arrows of the Almighty find their mark in me, and their poison soaks into my spirit: God's onslaughts wear me down.' (6.4)*

Job was not the only one to have a problem with the body. Calamity and suffering circle the Earth, and raise moral questions for people of all faiths. *Hinduism*, for example, sees the human soul 'imprisoned' in the body, and repeatedly being reborn in different types of body. When the soul fails to fulfil the moral law in one incarnation, it must strive to live aright in order to secure a superior position in the next body. The *Gnostic* faith which flourished at the beginning of the Christian era saw the physical world as the creation of demonic powers, and as 'imprisoning' the human soul in the evil body. The soul needs secret *knowledge (Greek, 'gnosis')* to escape the body.

Another similar notion arises in response to suffering, namely, that pain is *punishment* for wrongdoing. The disobedient Israelites are threatened with divine retribution:

> *'I (God) will use up all my arrows on them:*
> *pangs of hunger, ravages of plague, and bitter pestilence.'*
> *(Deuteronomy 32.24)*

The Hebrew prophet, Amos, believed that this was God's way:

> *'It was I who withheld the heavy showers from you*
> *while there was still three months to the harvest...*
> *I struck you with black blight and red;*
> *I dried up your gardens and vineyards...*
> *yet you did not come back to me.' (Amos 4.7,9)*

(Is heavy rain, or drought, a *punishment* from God?)

In Jainism's 'Acaranga Sutra' sin and pain are linked: *'in birth, death, final liberation and the removal of pain, the results of sin are at work.'*

Kay Carmichael writes in 'A Dictionary of Pastoral Care': *'The Greek root* 'poine', *meaning* 'penalty' *from which the word* 'pain' *is derived implies that pain was seen as a consequence of wrongdoing.'* (p.180)

Yet there is in reality no necessary or universal connection between pain and sin, nor between calamity and immorality. Pain is in fact an essential facet of our physical and spiritual existence. We are fragile flesh and blood, nerves , senses and consciousness not unfeeling robots. That being so, we feel pain and pleasure.

Positively also pain has some value. Kay Carmichael again writes,

> *'Pain teaches us to avoid injury and thus improves our chances of survival. It can force us to rest and give our body the opportunity to use its powerful capacity to heal itself.'*
> *(ibid, p.180)*

All saints under the sun on Broadstairs beech?

As for wider calamities such as floods and plagues, which inflict suffering, such afflictions are part of the complex systems of the Earth and its animal life, which have beneficial as well as ill consequences, but act irrespective of human sin or virtue. We recall Jesus' saying:

'God causes the sun to rise on good and bad alike, and sends the rain on the innocent and the wicked.' (Matthew 5.45)

Notwithstanding the fact of no necessary connection between suffering and sin, it is also a fact that sometimes they *are* linked. Guilt can cause worry and stress, which in turn lead to loss of appetite, sleepless nights and bodily exhaustion. Gluttony, alcohol, tobacco and drug-addiction can lead to diseases of the lungs, liver, heart and so on, each involving pain. Carelessness can ignite devastating forest fires. The use of chemicals can mutilate the soil or toxify rivers.

Over-cropping or deforestation can turn land into an unproductive dust bowl or desert. Sin *can* lead to suffering. Our physical life on Earth, in summary, can become either by natural causes or by human fault a *'vale of tears'!*

'A PLEASURE-DOME DECREED'

William Wordsworth draws our attention to the *sweet* side of life.

'O evil day! if I were sullen while Earth
herself is adorning this sweet May-morning;
And the children are culling on every side in
a thousand valleys far and wide fresh
flowers; while the sun shines warm..'

And lyrics from the musical, *'The Sound of Music'*, add the countless pleasures of our place in the physical world:

'Raindrops on roses, whiskers on kittens,
bright copper kettles and warm woolen
mittens,
silver white winters that melt into spring:
these are a few of my favourite things.'

Such pleasure has the same general origin as pain, namely, that it arises from our human physique and spirit: our flesh and blood, nerves, senses and consciousness. Furthermore, like pain, there is no necessary or universal connection between virtue and pleasure. Is the scent of a rose or the 'sound of a merry organ' morally good or bad? Further still, can we put a hairbreadth between pleasure and enjoyment, so that we may argue that we ought not to enjoy pleasure? No! May we not approve the view of Aristotle:

'...that people do best what they most enjoy doing, and that therefore in certain cases a person's relish for a given form of activity is evidence

that he or she is morally wise in adopting it.'

(D. M. Mackinnon in "A Dictionary of Christian Ethics")

Has not God, in short, long before Kublai Khan, ordained this earthly home as a *'pleasure-dome'* for his creatures?

Pleasure however can pose moral problems to us. The exquisite pleasure of eating and drinking can, when uncontrolled, turn into a compulsion with devastating results. The excessive pursuit of pleasure can turn a man into a 'playboy' lacking responsibility for his own and other people's lives.

Pleasure is good, but to vary a saying of Jesus: LIFE IS MORE THAN PLEASURE. Pleasure is to be relished, but, when needed, curbed for our own good.

WHERE IS GOD IN THIS BITTER-SWEET WORLD?

A TV documentary described the activity of American Christian evangelists in a village in Russia. As they commended faith in God, a young mother with a partially-sighted boy answered bitterly, *'What has God ever done for me?'*

Where is God when I am on a 'bed of pain' in this 'vale of tears'? The Russian woman's bitterness echoed the attitude of Job. Part of Job's answer is the ability to view his pain and trouble within the wider reality of the world he inhabits, and importantly, the world God has made.

The epic of *Job* has God saying:

'Where were you when I laid the earth's foundations?
Tell me if you know and understand...
Who supported the sea at its birth,
when it burst in flood from the womb?'
(Job 38.4,8)

All the universe is of God's making, and wherever I am in the world God is there with me in every circumstance, including pain. And pain, as we have noted, is an essential aspect of my body's vital sensitivity.

RAZOR-BLADES IN MY THROAT

THE worst pain I have ever known was a symptom of glandular fever. I endured this pain in my throat for five days. My daughter, Lois, who had suffered similarly, described the condition as 'like having razor-blades in your throat'! The excruciating pain was so severe that I frequently cried out for relief. Yet I can testify that I felt I was not alone; God was with me, comforting my soul, even though my body suffered. Milk, supplied by my wife, and healing spray, administered by the doctor, then soothed away the condition.

'When pain is to be borne', wrote C. S. Lewis, (quoted in 'Living Quotations for Christians') 'a little courage helps more than much knowledge, a little human sympathy more than much courage, and the least tincture of the love of God more than all.'

Blind Helen Kellar gave to God *'deep thanks that he set in my darkness the lamp of faith.'*

God is with us in suffering and in joy, loving, comforting, and giving courage to us whom he has set in this world.

> *TRULY, pain and pleasure are inevitable in God's overall plan which is to create people, who can feel and choose and love.*

THE MORAL WORLD - THE THIRD DIMENSION - DEALINGS WITH OTHER HUMAN BEINGS

THE basic question we have to answer here is: *'What is a human being worth?'*

Some soldiers of the First World War came to the conclusion that human life was cheap! Men were no more than 'cannon-fodder'. Today every terrorist bomb that kills someone shows how some people estimate other people.

The poet, Edward Fitzgerald, regarded our life as futile:

> *'One thing is certain, and the Rest is Lies;*
> *the flower that once has blown for ever dies...*
> *and this was all the Harvest that I reap'd -*
> *I came like water, and like wind I go.'*

If it is true that we are cheap, even worthless, it is logical to treat other people just how we wish, and certainly with neither respect nor love.

Such an estimate of a human being shows ignorance, willful or not, of the infinite marvel and value of our life. The Hebrew Psalmist over two millennia ago wrote in awe of God's creature *(Psalm 139.13-4)*

> *'You it was who fashioned my inward parts;*
> *you knitted me together in my mother's womb.*
> *I praise you, for you fill me with awe;*
> *wonderful you are, and wonderful your works.'*

Jesus affirms the value of each human life when he befriends, heals and converses with the frailest and most despised people. We remember Jesus' words: *'As for you, even the hairs of your head have all been counted.' (Matthew 10.30)*

C. G. Jung in the 20th century gives a psychologist's assessment of the worth of a human being (Memories and Reflections, p.18):

> *'Life has always seemed to me like a plant that lives on its rhizome. Its true life is invisible, hidden in the rhizome. The part that appears above*

ground lasts only a single summer. Then it withers away... Yet I have never lost a sense of something that lives and endures underneath the eternal flux. What we see is the blossom, which passes. The rhizome remains.' (Memories and Reflections, p18)

There is more to everyone we see than meets the eye! Robert Burns extols the 'rhizome-value' in every man and woman:

'For a' that and a' that, our toils obscure and a' that,
The rank is but the guinea's stamp, the man's the gowd for a' that.'

WHEN we realise the full worth of each person, we then respect them and act accordingly. We take to heart Jesus' call to treat others as we should like them to treat us; to love our neighbour as we love ourselves: my neighbour being - as shown in the parable of the Good Samaritan - any one we deal with of any nation in the world. Such a high estimate of people implies more: we act towards them as much for their sake as for our own. We do not care for people to gain a reward, but to help *them*. That is the highest morality. Don Cupitt, as we have noted, called this action *'disinterested love'*. This is a *basic principle* of our moral life.

HONESTY - INSIDE AND OUT

IF *love* is a basic principle, then it has a 'twin', called *'honesty'*. *'To thine own self be true',* wrote Shakespeare, *'and it shall follow as the night the day thou canst not be false to any man.'* Jesus agreed when he exposed the human fault of *hypocrisy* (the Greek word in the New Testament, meaning *acting* - pretending to be one kind of person, when really I am quite different). 'Be yourself', we are often urged. Be honest!

How does such honesty work out? If, for example, I know that I must protect my skin from sunburn on a hot day by wearing a hat and applying sun-block cream, then I don't pretend through laziness that I don't need protection. I act on what I know - and am saved from burning! I am true to myself.

Truth inside leads quite naturally to honesty outside. Honesty is one of the vital keys to open up strong human relationships.- in marriage, society, business and politics. To be honest is to create trust. People can rely on us to do the job we promised. When through long experience it is said of a spouse or a trader *'his word is his bond',* then that marriage or business is solid, reliable. Dishonesty is the wrecker of any relationship or enterprise.

Jesus with emphasis rightly advises: *'Let your "yes" mean "yes"!' (Matthew 5.37)*

PEOPLE BEHAVING BADLY

WE face another issue of our dealings with others, when *they treat us badly,* or let us down. Our impulse then is to be offended and to 'repay in kind'. The Krajina Serbs, stoned by Croats in Sisak, vowed:

'We'll bring back hell to the Croats. Vengeance, that's what most of these people have on their minds.'

The great drawback of 'paying in kind', of vengeance, is to make matters worse; to add to the sum of human misery; to aggravate and maybe break completely good human relations; and ultimately to cause the outbreak of war and its devastation.

But is there a better way of dealing with bad behaviour?

YES, THERE IS! Jesus described it

'LOVE your enemies and pray for your persecutors; only so can you be children of your heavenly Father, who causes the sun to rise on good and bad alike, and sends the rain on the innocent and the wicked.' (Matthew 5. 44-5)

Here there is at the very least the possibility not to make relations worse, and even to repair them!

This *basic principle* is also finely stated by the apostle, Paul:

'Never pay back evil for evil... Do not let evil conquer you, but use good to conquer evil.' (Romans 12.17,21)

SUCH , then, are our basic principles. Our next Parts will apply them to our dealings with people in our *Family, Nation and World-wide.*

MAKING SENSE OF LIFE - BOOK THREE

GOD AND THE MORAL WORLD

Part Two

Family Life

Family Album
Top - Autor's maternal grandparents (left) & author's parents (right).
Centre - author Malcolm and wife Kathleen.
Bottom - daughter Lois and son-in-law Mark with Jonathan

THE FAMILY IS THE BASIC 'BUILDING-BLOCK' OF HUMANKIND WORLD-WIDE

IT was right to begin our view of *God and the Moral World* by looking at *Basic Principles.* It is equally right to commence the application of those principles by dealing with *FAMILY LIFE.*

Why? Because the family is the *building-block* on which community, nation and global society is founded. The family could also be likened to a *cell of a body*, each cell related to others, and multiplying and growing in strength and ability as they interact.

So, the philosopher, George Santayana, wrote:

> *'The family is one of nature's masterpieces.'*

How true that is we discover when a family relationship breaks down.

THE DELINQUENT ELEPHANTS

A cull of elephant herds in southern Africa led to a number of the young being separated from their parents, and transported to other game-reserves. The result was that several of these young ones became 'delinquent'. They showed aggressive behaviour, including one attack on a tourist vehicle and the killing of a ranger who attempted intervention. The separation of parents and young was seen to be a mistake, because parents oversee their young and correct them when they go wrong. This discipline is part of the wider bonds of family interaction and emotion, which affect the character and behaviour of the young elephants.

THE break-up of a family points up the qualities of a stable family, 'nature's masterpiece'. What is its secret?

THE FAMILY'S SECRET LIES IN GOD

God's nature is *love,* and God imparts love to his creatures:

> *LOVE as* affection - *caring for and delighting in a child;*
> *LOVE as* respect - *for the rules of good behaviour;*
> *LOVE* determined *to practise caring and correcting bad behaviour.*
> *God's love is 'implanted' in every living creature.*

The love, 'implanted' in God's creatures has two aspects:

Physical, Instinctive Love

This is found in the love between parent and offspring in many animal species. A species of the *African hornbill* may make 30 or 40 trips in an hour to bring a single food item each time in its bill to feed the young in the nest. That is physical and instinctive love.

So also a human mother suckles her baby, cuddles and plays with the child, washes and dresses it.

Similarly, the love between adult inter-sexual partners from the first kiss of 'young-love' to the intimacy of intercourse , commonly called, 'making love', is 'doing what comes naturally', a physical, instinctive, God-given aspect of *love.* This physical, instinctive activity contributes to the bonding and stability of the family: indeed it is vital for a strong and happy family. But this is just part of the 'secret' of the 'masterpiece'.

Spiritual, Deliberate Love

This is the other part of the 'secret'. The life of the elephant family reveals a *love* beyond the physical and instinctive. The disciplining by the parent-elephants of their young shows the spiritual and deliberate aspect of love. Similarly after the initial tending of the human infant, there begins spiritual, deliberate concern. The child is by turns encouraged and curbed in its conduct (see further, pp. 96-97), and aided to education and friendships with peers.

The author's parents encouraged him in making friendships with his peers by welcoming them into the home and supporting activities. From left: Geoff Gaunt (Geologist), Brian Nowell (Civil Servant), The Author, Geoff Shaw (Auditor), Garry Burleigh (RAF). From 12 years to 70 they have kept in touch when possible.

At their best, parents have the ambition that their child will grow up to be a decent and happy man or woman; a person with moral and spiritual strength, and care for others. Also the relationship *between husband and wife* reaches into the realm of the spiritual and deliberate. Both wish to share more than a bed and a meal-table. They want to be together maybe watching TV, at a concert, touring, in church. Their targets reach far into the loving purpose of God for a man and a woman 'joined together in holy matrimony'. What are those targets?

THE FAMILY'S TARGETS

THESE are set out in a typical Christian Wedding Service, which we shall use as a framework.

TO LOVE **-** The description of *love (see Part 1)* as *affection, respect, humility and determination* applies here.

Affection - The target is to keep the 'flame' of liking and delighting in one's partner 'burning brightly' by asking for the *'white-heat of God's love'*. God is the source of affection, which is the 'spice' of marriage and the family.

Respect/Honour - The target is to realise always that the spouse has the basic human rights of safety of the body - safe from wife- or husband-battering and from rape. Each also is entitled to freedom of thought, which may be expressed in independent ideology, politics or religion. Furthermore, the equal dignity of woman and man before God is to be expressed in listening to each other and making decisions which affect the couple *together.*

Humility - The target is to be humble enough to admit and confess when I have wronged my partner; to forgive when I have been hurt; and for there to be mutual acceptance of apologies. Robert Quillen wrote: *'A happy marriage is the union of two good forgivers.'*

Determination The target is to 'work' at my marriage, realising that, as with all facets of life, *work* makes a difference: *'Whatever task lies to your hand, do it with might.' (Ecclesiastes 9.10)* An essential component of *determination* is perseverance, well put in the song popular in the early 20th century:

> *I'll be loving you always... not for just an hour,*
> *not for just a day, not for just a year, but always.'*

TO COMFORT. *'You never know what a day may bring forth.'* So we read in *Proverbs 27.1* That is true of our marriage. One day I was in the bathroom; my wife in the bedroom. Suddenly a loud, piercing scream came from the bedroom. My wife had pulled a drawer too far out , only for it to fall on her toes (an x-ray showed two of them to be broken). How Kathleen needed *comfort* then! *'What a day may bring forth'!* How many more unforeseen traumas will the years of marriage bring! The years may contain really serious trouble: the death of a child; a fatal accident; redundancy; the senility of a parent; all in all many occasions of the need for one partner to comfort the other. Many a marriage will bring the partners to the years of the menopause, involving depression, with a need for patience and presence, listening and sharing. (Books by Dr. Claire Weekes, published by Angus & Robertson, are helpful here.)

Old-age may call for a load of comfort! The word *comfort* means 'with strength', and each spouse needs to be *strong* to help the other every day, every year. The source of strength is the mighty God, *'whose matchless power is ever new and ever young'. (Isaac Watts' hymn, 'Awake our souls, away our fears..)*

FOR BETTER, FOR WORSE. We have in marriage the 'Jack Spratt Syndrome: *'Jack Spratt would eat no fat, and his wife would eat no lean!'*

This is true to life! Husband hates the smell of vinegar, onions, fish or sprouts... wife relishes them all! But these are relatively minor 'irritants'. The fact is that never shall one find an ideal or 'carbon-copy' partner: the paragon spouse doe not exist! Each partner has a 'better' and 'worse' side. The 'happy couple' on the wedding day both still wear 'L-plates'! Each has learning and growing-up in the 'training-course' of marriage to complete; each has the word,

IMPERFECTION, writ large on the image of the partner *and* imprinted on his or her own character. Equally each one, realising this fact, is challenged to work at 'sand-papering' the rough edges of his or her own character - the impatience, bad-temper, laziness or selfishness - with the aim of truly loving the other. Thus they can turn the 'worse' that they find into the 'better'!

FOR RICHER, FOR POORER. The wealth or poverty of the family is partly in the hands of the father and mother in their skill, business-sense and industriousness. So, in order to 'keep' each other and their family the target is to do one's best in using and developing those abilities. Partly of course the family is at the mercy of trade, recession or even war. When this results in being 'richer' or 'poorer', wealth must be kept as servant, not master, of the family, bearing in mind two sayings:

> *'Though wealth increases, do not set your heart on it.'*
> *(Psalm 62.10)*
> *'Better a dish of vegetables if love goes with it*
> *than a fattened ox eaten amid hatred.' (Proverbs 15.17)*

Most important of all however is the decision by husband and wife to hold their wealth in common: money and property is not 'mine', but 'ours': in practice joint bank-accounts are held, with minor agreed and equal amounts extracted as 'spends' for each spouse. Again, decisions about income and expense are openly discussed and made *together.* Thus is family stability securely founded, regarding wealth.

IN SICKNESS AND IN HEALTH. As the bride and groom stand side-by-side at the wedding, she perhaps an aerobics fanatic and he a six-foot sixteen-stone rugby player, sickness will probably be the last thing on their mind: this clause in their vows may seem to be quite academic!

Even so they will be most fortunate if over the next 20 or 40 years they may not have to take this vow very seriously. Suddenly one night he begins to feel sick; the next hours see repeated bouts of vomiting and diarrhoea. 'You've got a virus', decides the doctor. Some time later comes the day when she slips a disc, leaving her with acute pain, restricted movement and a period of traction or an operation in hospital. Later still, early one morning he finds the 'room beginning to spin'; he tries to stand up, but cannot! Alarm for both husband and wife; the call for the doctor and treatment for meniere's disease. Yet later, she suddenly says, 'Don't leave me on my own'. 'Why?' he asks, not understanding the panic and deep depression that often comes with a woman's menopause. It is at such times that each partner definitely needs the other, and the target is to be available to act as nurse and comforter, and when necessary to call quickly for professional medical attention to restore the stricken one to health.

TILL DEATH PARTS

'Love alters not with his brief hours and weeks,
but bears it out even to the edge of doom.
If this be error, and upon me prov'd,
I never writ, nor no man ever lov'd.'

Shakespeare sets this target of marriage in a Sonnet. Each partner desires to make a long-term, indeed a permanent commitment to the other. A marriage is worth very little without such commitment. Married people- as a couple and as parents need to be able to count on each other to be available for each other. It is not a matter of taking each other for granted, but it is about being able to trust each other to be faithful and reliable day by day and year after year in all the changing activities, with their toils and joys gladly shared.

This committed activity of the family was defined millennia ago by Ruth in the Book of her name *(Ruth 1.16,17):*

'Where you go, I will go, and where you stay I will stay.
Your people shall be my people, and your God my God.
Where you die, I will die, and there I will be buried.
I swear a solemn oath before the Lord your God:
nothing but death shall divide us.'

TO SURROUND CHILDREN WITH LOVE. The ingredients of love, operative between wife and husband, apply also in the parent-child relationship.

Affection As the parents like and enjoy the child, he or she will receive the power to like and enjoy himself or herself and other people. The child will grow in self-confidence and happiness.

Respect The child has the right to respect for its body from those upon whom it depends, including the provision of food. Equally the child's mind is nourished by the parents answering its questions. Thereby the child is taught to care for its body and to think for itself and to respect other people.

Humility Mum and Dad will be heroes to their child, but even they with their imperfections will not 'get it right' all the time. When they are able to say, 'Sorry', to their child, they will be the better able to assist the child to admit faults.

Determination A child is a human being 'in the raw': the child's early years are a time of *'trial and error'!* Hence, the parents' love for their child will be sorely tried, and strength, patience and perseverance of the highest order are necessary. The parents can pray for the patience of God in their efforts.

Children learn what they live

IF a child lives with criticism, she learns to condemn.
If a child lives with hostility, he learns to fight.
If a child lives with ridicule, she learns to be shy.
If a child lives with shame, he learns to feel guilt.
If a child lives with tolerance, she learns to be patient.

If a child lives with encouragement, he learns confidence.
If a child lives with praise, she learns to appreciate.
If a child lives with fairness, he will be just.
If a child lives with security, she will learn to have faith.
If a child lives with approval, he will learn to like himself.
If a child lives with acceptance and friendship,
he or she learns to find love in the world.

TO INSTRUCT AND CORRECT CHILDREN. 'Camp is the Scoutmaster's great opportunity', we were taught. Being with the boys all day, perhaps for a week, was the chance to teach them the skills of looking after themselves and of living and sharing with other boys. That was the aim of Scouting.

The family home is all the more the *parents'* 'great opportunity' to instruct their children in the multitude of skills required for a lifetime, from tying shoelaces to brushing hair, from crossing a road to buying the first motor car.

A most important element in the parents' instruction will be unconscious example. The psychologist, Judy Harris, estimates the influence of a child's peers as greater than its parents. Yet the influence of the parents is still very strong. The parents' opportunity to mould the knowledge and behaviour of their child is their presence with the child hourly, daily, from birth. The child sees their actions, hears their words, and feels their attitude and mood. (See *'Children Learn What They Live', above)'My Mum and Dad are looking for a half-decent caravan'*, said a small boy. Was this not just the 'echo' of his parents' words? Equally influential is the more conscious instruction by the parents.

The 'Traffic-Lights' Strategy

We saw this 'strategy' in action (in *Part* 1) within the soul.

'Go', 'Pause', and 'Stop' also operates in the parents' education of a child. How important this is!

'GO'

A child possesses vigorous abilities and desires in body, mind and soul. These should be developed by parents: *'Can I learn to swim? ride a bicycle? join the Brownies? have a book of prayers?'* How important, if the parents have the means, to respond, *'Yes, go for it!'* How important also for the parents to take the initiative; to go for a walk in the country, to read some poetry to the child: overall, to open up the world of knowledge and experience to their offspring. So, the child can sprout a positive inclination to life. He or she will grow in skills and capability, and will learn by example to take initiative and be pro-active.

'PAUSE'

''Look before you leap', is often good advice to a child. He or she needs to be taught how to *wait* sometimes until he or she is capable enough to do what only *appears* to be good right now.

By *waiting* the child will acquire the precious gift of patience, and learn that some of the most satisfying goals are only achieved by gradual, persevering labour.

'STOP'

'No' is a vital word in a child's instruction. 'No, Johnny, don't put the knife in your mouth!' 'No. I said only one more biscuit after that good dinner you've eaten and I mean it!' 'No. You have plenty of Lego at present. We can't afford any more just now, anyway.'

By saying 'No' on the right occasion the parent not only prevents trouble for the child and the parents, but also develops the most precious and often saving capability of *self-control.*

WHEN BITS 'DROP OFF' THE FAMILY

CHILDREN GROW UP! Before you know it, the babe-in-arms is in the arms of a 'young lover'!

Very soon the unsteady toddler is confidently running off far and wide. Mary Howarth, a mother of five girls aged two to ten in Oldham, said, *'I die a thousand deaths'*. She referred to the girls leaving her sight and hold for various reasons and varied lengths of time.

Drawing the line between responsible watching-over, and encouraging a child to venture out into the street and district on its own is difficult. A gradual 'loosening of the apron-strings' is advisable. My mother, in my teenage years, allowed me to go cycling with my peers. We would begin by travelling about three miles up the coast. Next we made a round-trip of over thirty miles from our Morecambe home to Windermere. Then, Youth Hostelling holidays gradually extended from three days to ten, taking us from the Yorkshire Dales to North Wales, London and Northern Ireland (in the peaceful days of 1947).

I am always grateful for the calculated risk my mother and those my friends took, enabling me to learn how to look after myself and find out at first hand about the wider world. It fitted me soon to leave my home-town for Manchester!

The supremely vital factor to understand as 'bits fall off' the family is that each member of the family has the great advantage of living in a mixture of two spheres of existence - the communal (family) and the individual. This mixture can have a 'downside', leading to conflict between family ties and individual freedom. That happens whenever either seeks to dominate, and especially in the time of growing self-assertion in the puberty period. However, each member of the family, parent or offspring, needs to attempt to balance the two spheres, because both the security of togetherness and the adventure of independence contribute to the fully-rounded life. A facet of this balance is cited in *Genesis 2.24: 'a man leaves his father and mother and attaches himself to his wife, and the two become one.'*

Finally, it is good experience to be able to enjoy the advantage of both family belonging and personal freedom, even when a man or woman has left the ancestral home to marry and create a new family. The tie of love through at least three generations need not -and should not- be severed. The 'bits added on' - in-laws and grandchildren - can furthermore be a boon and blessing to the whole family!

THE FAMILY'S CHALLENGERS

THE FAMILY does not live in a cocoon. Husband and wife are not confined within monastic walls. The milkman calls. The girl in the office glides by like a 'phantom of delight'. Also, the first flush of courting and newly-wedded bliss fade into the 'light of common day'. The excitement of newness subsides into the routine of domesticity.

It is further a fact of great importance that every human life alters as it grows. To be human is to develop, whether quickly or slowly. Circumstances and experiences, success and failure, excitement and boredom, affect our attitudes, satisfactions and views. It would then be unlikely that wife and husband have the same outlook ten, twenty or more years after marriage. There is much likelihood that they *could* 'grow apart' with time.

Another noteworthy factor, already mentioned is the imperfection of each partner in a marriage. If such faults, at first tolerated, become deeper and barely to be endured, they may tear the couple apart.

A THIRD PARTY

THE onset of family routine or growing apart or worsening faults, each can prise an opening for a *'third party'* to step onto the scene. A challenge is presented to a husband or wife: a new, exciting experience with a third person who seems to match, with more in common than the humdrum or estranged spouse; one who has a virtue that the faulty partner lacks (how very likely!) arrives. 'The other man's grass is always greener!' This third party is a doughty rival!

How can the marriage and the family withstand the onslaught?

A deeper love for the spouse than for a third party *alone* can defy the challenge: a love deep enough to cherish the 'routine of domesticity'; a love broad enough to bridge the changes in the partner's attitudes, satisfactions and views; a love understanding enough to be patient with the spouse's shortcomings; a love so lively that it can bring fresh excitement into married, family life. Such love will overcome, as was expressed again in Shakespeare's Sonnet:

'Love is not love which alters when it alteration finds,
or bends with the remover to remove:
O, no! it is an ever-fixed mark,
that looks on tempests and is never shaken;
it is a star to every wandering bark,
whose worth's unknown, although his height be taken.'

WORK

THE second challenge has in principle the moral justification that a third party lacks. Most husbands and/ or wives have no alternative but to go out to work; one or other must be the 'breadwinner', and generally the better 'fist' one makes of a job the more surely will 'bread' be on the family table. Further, no generalisation can be made about the time or the physical or mental effort that the work may require. It could entail overtime, labour in another area, or duties with some danger. Such situations make a challenge to time shared with the spouse and children, and ask for understanding. The target is to balance the commitment to the family and to the work, yet seeking the maximum time and care for the family.

SERVICE TO THE COMMUNITY

LIKE a plant a family cannot live in isolation. The adult members work with other people in factory, shop or field; they buy from and sell to other families; they eat out at a cafe or hotel and so on. The children go to a nursery, a school, a college, uniformed organisation, a gym club; buy toys or borrow library- books. All the family is served by water, gas, and electrical engineers, and live in a house, a street, a town, serviced by power stations and served by local authorities.

All this activity has to be organised, and the more people who give time, thought and energy to this, the better service will be rendered to all the citizens. And who are these people who serve? Members of families!

It happens then that another challenger to family life is *community service*. As with work, there is moral justification for a Mum or Dad to serve as a town councillor, school governor, scout leader, treasurer for the local institute for the blind or Church Elder. There is, though, as with work, the need to be alert to the danger that one could become a 'bigamist' -'married to the council/scouts/church', and 'separated' from the family. Again, the aim is to hold the right balance.

LEISURE ACTIVITIES

'All work and no play makes Jack a dull boy!'

'What is this life, if full of care we have no time to stand and stare!'

'Leisure'; 'diversion'; 'break'; 'recreation'; 'relaxation': all these words spell out the value of a time without work. This is precious in itself, and also supplies new renewed strength and alertness, necessary when work is resumed. Once again this challenge is justified.

'Just the ticket', then, if both husband and wife love to sing in the local operatic society or play mixed-doubles at tennis or share a taste for food in a Chinese restaurant. No less justified it may be for a Mum to 'get away from it all' at a women' s institute aerobics group, or Dad to relax (!) at a weight-training class.

The challenge comes to the family if the leisure activity becomes an obsession or an indulgence, preferred to being with members of the family. An early assessment of priorities is necessary here as with the other challengers.

THE FAMILY'S PURPOSE

'GOD IS LOVE
and anyone who lives in love lives in God,
and God lives in him.'
(1 John 4.16)

GOD'S purpose is that family relationships
between wife and husband, parents and children
should partake in this loving.
So writes the author of Genesis (1.27):
'GOD created human beings in his own image;
... male and female he created them.'
LOVE between God and ourselves, is, for Jesus,
the norm - *the greatest command of life.*
So, marriage and the family are part of the fulfilling of God's purpose,
the incarnation of God's love.

THE FAMILY'S GREAT ALLIES

GOD is the family's great ally. God not only makes marriage and the family; God also sustains each member in the ongoing enterprise. A human partner's love is backed up by God's love through faith and prayer. When challengers would break up the family, the Great Ally will alert the conscience of the one attacked, so that he or she is prepared for an assault, and will give the courage and love, when asked, to resist and strengthen the bond of marriage and the family.

THE FAMILY'S JESTER. 'IT can happen in the best-regulated households!' Husband pulls down the garage-door on his wife's head: not on purpose, but in the rush during a hailstorm! Wife hosepipes husband with water: not with malice-aforethought, but trying to avoid a wasp! It happens all the time! And what the family needs is a *'jester'*; to make you laugh at the mishaps and the 'worse' side of married life. Many otherwise sad and fracturing episodes are transformed by the 'jester' *a sense of humour!*

This also is the gift of the God of love and *joy.*

GRANDPARENTS, AUNTS AND UNCLES. 'They also serve...' And baby-sitting is only one of their 'labours of love'. Most important is the experience, advice and wisdom by which they back-up and enrich the younger generations. Mum and Dad are sometimes 'rushed off their feet', but grandparents have (sometimes) time and to spare to consider their offspring's problems, and to listen to the grandchild's news and answer the questions. This author is ever grateful to grandmother, Sarah Jane Hill, who 'had time' for him, told him to 'wash behind your ears', and taught him to reverence God and how to pray. Equal thanks go to his great-aunt, Annie Sutcliffe, who so cared for him as to pay for his early secondary education.

Such allies are invaluable to hard-pressed families. So, we end this Part in the style of Psalm 103:

> *'BLESS the Lord, my soul:*
> *bless God for husbands and wives'*
> *sons and daughters, grandparents, aunts and uncles.*
> *With all my being I bless God's holy name.'*

A FOOTNOTE ON DIVORCE

WE have set out in this Part the 'targets' for family life including the desirability of husband and wife committing each to the other 'till death parts'. We also granted that marriage has formidable challengers, but still upheld the ability to outface the rivals. We acknowledge all this and yet we have to accept that our human attitudes and actions are far from *ideal*, and that this certainly applies to married life. Thus, a couple may commit themselves to marriage with the full intention that the union should be permanent. However, serious flaws in the character of either spouse may subsequently develop, leading one or the other to act with extreme physical or mental cruelty toward the partner, or to become repeatedly unfaithful. These are just a couple of examples of many instances of the complete breakdown of the marriage relationship. The question then arises: *'Is it right that the marriage be annulled - or is it not?*

Christians have predominantly been guided to answer by reference to the Bible. Yet again, however, Biblical guidance is not consistent. It is implied in the *Book of Deuteronomy (24.1-4)* that divorce is permissible when a husband finds *'some indecency'* in his wife

The Gospel according to Mark (10.10-12) contrarily reports Jesus as objecting to divorce completely. Yet another Gospel has Jesus make an exception to the ban on divorce, that is *'unchastity' (Matthew 5.32).* The immediate cause of Jesus' reported sayings, it is suggested, (Book *Two, Part 2, p.2-22)* is his concern for the rights of the wife. Still, the difference between *Mark* and *Matthew* require us to make up our own judgement on the question.

We ought then to consider Jesus' prevailing understanding of and compassion toward our human imperfections. We must ask ourselves:

> *'Is it compassionate to insist that a spouse should be forbidden to annul a marriage with a persistently cruel or neglectful or adulterous partner and subsequently also to forbid remarriage?'*

JESUS' enduring principle is
mercy and forgiveness and a
fresh start for us all!

This principle is extremely appropriate to the demanding responsibilities and potential for tragic breakdown which marriage entails. When all efforts to achieve reconciliation have been tried, and failed, divorce and remarriage are part of the mercy and new life that Jesus affords to imperfect human beings.

MAKING SENSE OF LIFE - BOOK THREE

GOD AND THE MORAL WORLD

Part Three

Society-Economy-Nation

SOCIETY-ECONOMY-NATION

ONE of the most bizarre incidents in my youth was sitting on the front seat of a bus for the short ride from my grandmother's house to my home, clutching on my lap a huge lump of coal wrapped in newspaper!

How often have you witnessed such a sight recently? Perhaps it was an odd scene even in the late 1940's during the severe rationing of coal.

Yet, as the coal was wrapped up in newspaper, so the fact and wonder of human *society* is 'wrapped up' in that scene: the *family* is 'wrapped' inside the wider *society.*

My grandmother's mind had been informed and interested by the newspaper. The newspaper was a product of the reporters, editor and printers, who make up that wider society. My family home also was warmed by the coal, mined by men working at the coal-face 'somewhere in England'. Each of our bodies and minds are fed, warmed and enriched by others. Such is *society.*

SOCIETY AS A BLESSING

HUMAN SOCIETY IS UNSPEAKABLY BLESSED! It is an unfathomable reservoir to slake everyone's thirst: we drink of it moment by moment, day after day.

We may be apprised of this by the origin of many of our family *surnames.* We inherit the legacy of medieval society where surnames began. So, John the weaver became John Weaver, and Alan the shearer ended up as Alan Shearer.

Tom the sawyer - alias - Tom Sawyer

The distinct occupations that made up society gave us the names: Baker, Barber, Tyler, Thatcher, Paynter, Glazier, Draper, Tanner, Vintner, Spicer, Shepherd, Harper, Piper and Singer. Yet other names tell us how our lives are enhanced as people migrate from one district to another, inserting fresh blood and new ideas and stories. So we have surnames such as (the) Newman who came to the village, or the 'offcomer' who came from Middleton, or Milton, or from famous London or Edinburgh, not to mention the odd German or French.

Thus a community consists of individual human beings with distinct talents, living together and serving each other in their locality. A village or town receives new citizens who bring fresh ways, and help to build the potential for an efficient and fascinating *society.* This state of affairs was, as we saw in *Book Two,* the concern of Jesus as he stressed *both* the infinite value of the *individual human soul* and the collective worth of *human society.* We are *blessed*!

SOCIETY - TO BE OR NOT TO BE ?

WE have so far been praising *society.* Yet often it is spoken against. Why ? People singly or together can be oppressive - from the bully-boy ringleader of a gang through the local clique to the police-state. The criticism of society has many pretexts, which we shall try to unearth, and the attack on society can have a profound effect on our economy and politics, our nation and our world.

THE CHOICE OF ANARCHY

2400 years ago the Greek, Aristippus, taught that wise people must not give up their liberty to the state, and said that he did not desire to belong to the governing or governed class. He was an advocate of *anarchy* (Greek: 'no rule'). Leaping from ancient Greece to 19th century Russia, Bakunin demanded the destruction of the state - which he saw as an organ of oppression - by insurrection. He rejected political action. Sadder even than these spokesmen for anarchy are practitioners who have lived outside the law in much of the earth for most of human history, and are very much alive today.

Penny Lernoux, a journalist and resident in South America for many years summarised the situation in that continent in her book, *'Cry of the People (1980)'*:

> *'The well-to-do in Latin America live better than do the upper classes in the United States; they have platoons of servants, enormous estates, limousines, private airplanes, and yachts, and pay practically no taxes. This baronial style of life is still possible because the cornerstone of the colonial system remains intact - the law of the strongest.'*
> *(Page 20)*

Since Penny Lernoux wrote her book the ground-swell of anti-state opinion has surged in the USA. President Reagan adopted the rallying-cry, *'Get the government off our backs'*. The result was severe cutbacks in aid to the poorer citizens, and the fracture of society.

Britain also in the 1980s and early 1990s travelled some way along the road of anti-state, anti-society living. This was advocated by Prime Minister, Margaret Thatcher in her saying, *'There is no such thing as society. There are individual men and women and there are families.'* This is dangerous talk as far as society is concerned: supremely because it is plainly untrue - as demonstrated at the start of this *Part*.

Why did Margaret Thatcher utter such a falsity? We may give her credit for being the champion of the individual's sense of responsibility and habit of hard work, as against 'passing the buck' and sponging on other people. Bravo! But the debit side of her saying is its encouragement of all people whose 'creed' is self-first, insisting on their own way, and those who desire to opt-out of their community and accumulate wealth, regardless of the poverty of others. Such people are the true 'anti-social' ones, and we shall find the dire results of their anarchic ways when we proceed to look at economic affairs. Such attacks on the very concept *of society* and altruism - care for others - enfeebled social responsibility in Britain for many years.

But not only in Britain. As the Communist bloc of eastern Europe was moderating its regime in the late 1980s, 'Thatcherism', in triumphant mood, took up a 'mission' to 'roll back the frontiers of Socialism'. This was virtually 'pushing at an open door', and the Communist regimes fell like a 'pack of cards'. As the grip of the Communist governments loosened, all those who had resented the regime and desired to pursue their self-interest leapt to their liberation. They achieved a counter-revolution, reversing the Communist victory in Russia in 1917, and its dominance in eastern Europe following the war in 1945.

The history of this counter-revolution, not least in Russia, is a stark illustration of the title of this *Part, 'Society-Economy-Nation'.* The three words are hyphenated, indicating that society, economy and nation are three modes of human community which *merge* into one another. Thus, there has taken place - in Russia for example - firstly a disintegration of society. (The sense of belonging and mutual help has been replaced by self-interest.) This then merged in the 1990s into a free-market economy of the most antisocial and unfair type, with a free - for -all in profits, salaries, wages and prices, a most lax tax-system (estimated 50% of salaries 'paid under the table'), and a large black-market, high degree of corruption and protection-racketeering. Finally, the virility of the free-market battered down *state/national* government – as shown by the statement of Miranda Anichkina, referring to the Yeltsin regime between 1993 and 1997: *'There has not been a single plan for the restructuring of the economy during this Period.'* Another commentator concludes: *'Russia today (1997) is a political and economic disaster.'* That this is no dramatic exaggeration is shown in the estimated £4 billion unpaid salaries and pensions to valuable workers such as teachers and miners, and in children abandoned by parents who cannot afford to feed them. A civil servant, Leonid Genin, tells of:

> *'...parents unemployed, drinking too much, and not giving enough attention to their children... delinquency increased 10 times... growing problems of crime, drug-use, and Aids among teenagers'.*

This is what happens when people choose *anarchy:* equality of treatment ends; the 'law of the strongest' rules; the weakest are trampled upon. This situation in Russia - a broken society-economy- nation - is repeated in nation after nation world-wide.

THE CHOICE OF SOCIETY

PEOPLE have a choice other than *anarchy.* They can choose *society.* It may seem illogical to 'choose society'. We can in one sense no more make such a choice than choosing to be born or the colour of our skin.

Yet in another sense we can 'choose society' - with its economy and state system. Just as we can not only live on the earth, but also *choose* to appreciate our life here, so we can choose to *appreciate* society and make the effort to invigorate society.

One of the most explicit instances of the *choosing* of society-economy-nation in history is that of the HEBREWS under the leadership of Moses and his successors.

Here it was a case of God and the Hebrews making a mutual choice. The belief was as follows:

> *'(God says). If only you will now listen to me and keep my covenant, then out of all peoples you will become my special possession . . a kingdom of priests, my holy nation.' (Exodus 19.5,6)*
>
> *'Then Moses took the Book of the Covenant and read it aloud for the people to hear. They said, "We shall obey, and do all that God has said."'*
> *(Exodus 24.7)*

This basic commitment developed into ritual, economy and national life, described especially in the *Book of Leviticus, Chapters 16 & l9,* and in the *Books of Samuel and Kings.*

Jesus deepened appreciation of society as the 'kingdom of God', and reinvigorated it. (Book *Two, Part 2)* His followers lived within a *'new covenant'* - a fresh commitment - (See *Letter to the Hebrews 12.24),* and were *'constantly meeting to hear the apostles teach and to share the common life, to break bread, and to pray' (Acts of the Apostles 2.42).* Like their Hebrew ancestors they proceeded to ritual and economic activity.

> *'All the believers agreed to hold everything in common: they began to sell their property and possessions and to distribute to everyone according to his need. One and all they kept up their daily attendance at the Temple, and, breaking bread in their homes, they shared their meals with unaffected joy.'*
> *(Acts 2.44-6)*

The choice of *society* - and by implication - of *economy* and *nation* is first of all *God's choice,* and then *humankind's choice.* God has given us the blessing of *both* individuality and togetherness, and the key to a good society is the choice and affirmation of *both* blessings. We need to safeguard the bodily and spiritual requirements of each citizen, whilst we pursue the greatest good of the society-economy-nation.

How tragic it is when powerful men fail to grasp this need for *both* personal freedom *and* national welfare - as when Boris Yeltsin, Russian President, 1991-9, told the Chinese leadership, as his troops were slaughtering Chechen men, women and children in Grozny, that national sovereignty was more important than human rights. The same leader presided over the lavish embellishment of the Kremlin in Moscow whilst so many of his nation became street- beggars. Such gross injustice is not confined to Russia!

A society or kingdom, which has its ruler in a golden palace, and its citizens in filthy slums has missed its goal!

SO, we have the *choice: ANARCHY* - every man for himself; or *SOCIETY,* where we ensure, by law, that we treat others as we should like them to treat us. THE CHOICE IS OURS !

THE ECONOMY

WEALTH-CREATION

ANOTHER of Margaret Thatcher's notable sayings went: 'No *one would remember the Good Samaritan, if he'd only had good intentions. He had money as well."* What was the point of this remark? Probably to remind us that all the socially-desirable institutions such as schools, hospitals and homes for the elderly remain daydreams, if no one works in field and factory to produce the wealth. Someone in each family has to labour to 'bring home the bacon'. Someone has to rear the pigs, slaughter them and serve at the cooked-meat counter. A society-economy which is well-serviced needs the labour of an 'army' of workers, occupied in a myriad of often strange but vital ways. I have seen two men *creating wealth* simply by using a crowbar: one, all alone in the west of Ireland, quarrying building-stone; the other in a large factory in St.Helens, England, all the time breaking the unusable ends of a plate-glass conveyor-belt. From the down-to-earth farmer to the up-in-the-sky airline pilot, people everywhere are creating the wealth without which society-economy-nation would perish.

Through work we have money! We must, therefore, appreciate all people who create wealth - businessmen, managers, manual workers and skilled people, in agriculture or manufacture or services.

MONEY £ $ DM ¥

OUR society-economy has long left behind the arrangement whereby the quarryman 'brought home his bacon' by carting stone to the pig-farmer ! Money is much easier to deal with than barter. It is truly a precious tool for our economic life - as valuable as a net to a fisherman or a violin to a musician. The 'liquidity' of money is like the oil to the machine: it keeps a society's economy moving.

But a note of warning needs to be struck. *'The love of money is the root of all evils.' (1 Timothy 6.10)* Greed for money can make us hurt others - through lying, attacking and even killing them. Greed has blossomed in recent years, as shown in the exorbitant salaries, 'incentives' and 'golden handshakes' accrued by already rich people. These 'captains of industry' have, in the process, down-sized their work-forces; their gain has meant the loss of livelihood and hope of their fellows, and their example has inspired impressionable young people to deem 'making money' their chief aim in life. Jesus summed up the danger of the love of money:

'You cannot serve God and money.' (Matthew 6.24)

Money is a good servant, but a bad master'.

MARKET-FORCES

THE use of money in trading - or marketing - is beneficial to people only when there is fair competition. Then, prices of goods and services can be held in check and their quality can be increased. Yet market-forces can operate perversely, when used by bosses who maximize their profits by depressing wages or by cutting staff-numbers; or when there is no legal control over house-sale profiteering. Market-forces - like other forces - need to be kept under control. This is our responsibility as citizens - through our elected nation-state - as we shall see.

WEALTH-SHARING

AS surely as the Good Samaritan 'had money', and was probably a wealth-creator, he was also a *wealth-sharer* to the victim, who depended on him for survival. We have in this incident 'in a nutshell' the economic situation of practically the whole of human society around the world:
prosperity and poverty side by side.

The fact is that the state of economic affairs in Britain, where the biggest wealth-creators - 1% of the population - possess 18% of the total wealth of the nation, and the poorer 50% of the people own 8% of the wealth, is repeated in most of the world's nations. (Also compare with 1st century Palestine, p. 55). The situation plainly is one where a few people are immensely rich whilst many others are desperately poor. This, as Jesus emphasised, (Book Two, Part 2) is an affront to God's value of each human being - in need of 'daily bread'. If, of course, there was just not enough bread to go round, that could be a charge against the Creator, God ! But the facts are well put by Mahatma Gandhi:

'There is enough for everyone's need,
but not for everyone's greed.'

So, the most pressing challenge for our economy is to *distribute /share the wealth of the Earth fairly.* How can this be done ?

WAGES

WAGES is a good place to start in fair distribution. A prevalent question is: *'Can we afford a minimum wage?'* A prudent politician may ask that, but the question is 'out of court' in a nation that would base its economy on Christian, theological and moral grounds. Britain's resources *can* afford a decent minimum wage. (There is enough wealth/bread for everyone's need here.) This could be partly funded by employers and partly by increased taxes. Our diagrams (following) show up the results - for good or ill - by adopting or rejecting a minimum wage. The question should not be, 'Can we afford?', but, 'Have we the moral decency to share our wealth with poorly-paid workers?' Further, we ought not to regard this redistribution condescendingly as 'trickle-down', but as the right policy for a caring society-economy-nation.

Furthermore, as there is a case for a *minimum wage,* so there is for a *maximum wage* - at least until we have ended 'poverty-pay' in our nation. We should note here the selfishness and hypocrisy of people who oppose the minimum wage, because it will price workers out of a job, whilst they themselves justify their sky-high salaries, saying they are worth every penny. Who is pricing himself out of a job more? The one asking for £4 an hour (£10,000 a year) or the one demanding £60 an hour (£150,000 a year). It will be objected that having a maximum salary will kill incentive to excellent work, but let us ask ourselves:

> *'Would I put less into my work if I had a salary of £50,000, rather than £150,000?'*

Only the undedicated and greedy would reply, 'Yes'. It is best here to apply our general Christian principle: that our chief motive for all action and work is the love and service of others,

THE DETRIMENTAL CIRCLE

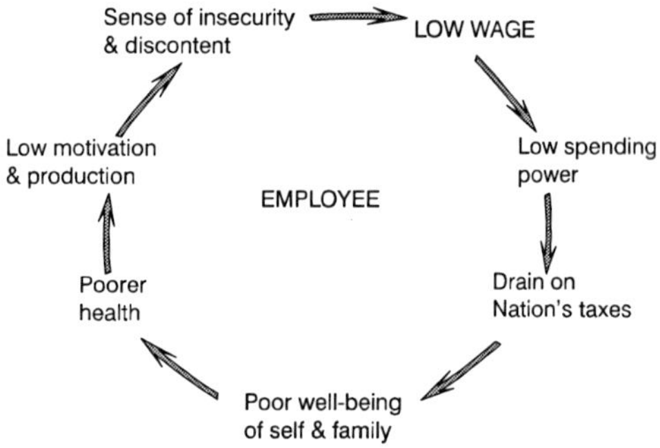

THE BENEFICIAL CIRCLE

which Jesus showed; loving service which is not interested primarily in rewards or perks, but in excellence of work.

Having established that principle, it is fair that in earning our living each worker should be paid according to hours spent in toil, and according to qualifications attained through study and/or experience. It will be best to calculate these differentials through mutual consultation by way of a national incomes policy.

It cannot be stressed too much to point this out:

fair remuneration for labour
is one of the most important means
of right wealth-sharing.

EMPLOYMENT

'TOP of our nation's agenda ought to be providing proper jobs.... We have become fatalistic, assuming that nothing can be done about mass unemployment...'

These are the words of David Sheppard, when Bishop of Liverpool. He spoke in advance of a Churches' essay on '*Unemployment and the Future of Work' (1997).* This betrays the emotion of a keen observer of the depressing situation in Merseyside, where in the 1990s various schemes of job-creation failed to provide the solid, long-term, decently-paid employment for so many people.

Having a job, which pays for daily bread is one of the most important 'planks' of a society-economy. This is so, firstly, because indeed it sustains the financial needs of the worker and the family. But employment, like love, is a 'many-splendoured thing'. As we saw, from the Slater to the Singer, a person can trade talent and effort for cash. At the same time, he or she can use and develop varied gifts in the service of society. I, an employee as a preacher, gazed one day in awe as a slater strolled easily up and down a pitched roof. I suppose he would have been in as much trepidation, had I called on him to preach a sermon in front of a congregation!

And there is still more benefit in employment, as Will Hutton writes in *'The State We're In', p.99:*

'... the rhythm of work gives life meaning. The achievement of new tasks, the acquisition of skills, and the social intercourse that is part and parcel of the work experience is not something human beings want to avoid; they want and need it.'

If employment is so beneficial, it is a priority for a Christian society - economy - nation so to plan projects of work, and dispose finance, as to effect as full employment as possible.

UNEMPLOYMENT

SHOULD all efforts to create jobs fail to supply, people unemployed should receive from a Christian state security against poverty and hunger; a payment capable of preserving their human dignity. It is especially cruel and negligent to berate and penalise jobless people, who are made so by market-forces, which have been designed to increase the wealth of the already-affluent.

RETIREMENT PENSIONS

PEOPLE who retire because of age become dependent on the wealth-creators. How may they best be financed ? The answer is: by a pension scheme as part of a welfare-state. This is well set out by Will Hutton in *'The State We're In', p.306:*

> *'The welfare state is a symbol of our capacity to act together morally, to share and to recognize the mutuality of rights and obligations that underpins all human association . . it has to be based on a series of income transfers between classes and generations underwritten by the recognition that social cohesion results from common endeavour, and is a good which benefits all.'*

A fair, sharing pension scheme involves each citizen paying, out of earnings, a pension contribution, later to be received. Such a basic contribution may be augmented by extra payments toward a state pension or by payments to a private insurance scheme. The rate of a state pension should be determined by the current national wages in order to maintain general fairness in society as a whole.

MONEY: ITS SAVING & INVESTMENT

JUST as money can be a mixed-blessing, so can the investment of money.

Suppose you or I were fortunate enough to have £100,000 at our disposal. We should have three broad options to take:-

1. *Put it all into the bank to gain interest -for a 'rainy day'.*
2. *Spend it all quickly, eg. buying a house.*
3. *Divide the amount into two - half in the bank, half in the house.*

Would not the third option be the wisest? It would certainly be the wisest for a nation's economy.

Will Hutton cites the British economy in the first years after the 2nd World

War, when governments encouraged investment in the aircraft and chemical industries, which long flourished as a result. *'Investment',* he writes, in *'The State We're In:*

> *'is the key motor of the economy's prosperity because it has a snowball effect, what Keynes called the multiplier. Investment is the part of national output which raises future productive capacity...' (p.242).*

For example -

INVESTMENT x MANUFACTURE x DOMESTIC GOODS x MORE INVESTMENT

Hutton further commends the creation of regional banks - as in Germany, which can help businesses with investment finance. Such banks have local knowledge of their customers, business strategies and future commercial viability. Banks and businesses thus have a sense of belonging to the cities and regions where they operate.

Investment in research and training is also important. Investigation and experimentation can improve existing products and create new ones in the economy, and the training of workers is a boost to them and their businesses.

Basically an economy beneficial to all the people requires the blend of saving for the future, and spending to increase business in the present.

TAXATION

'TAXES are the sinews of the state', said the Roman, Cicero.

This ancient institution, often reviled and avoided, truly does help to hold a civilized society together.

WHAT IF YOU HAD NO TAXES TO PAY?

NO COUNCIL TAX, NO INCOME TAX,
NO NATIONAL INSURANCE?
Why then, there would be no roads, no street-lamps,
no refuse-collection, no police-force, no fire-brigade,
no hospitals or clinics, no doctors or nurses,
no schools or universities or public libraries,
no environmental protection,
no courts, no parliament, no law and order !
When the people of a nation do not
share their resources, either through neglect
of taxation or widespread tax-evasion,
then they condemn themselves
to a poor quality of life -
to injustice, poverty and violence -
the breakdown of law and order.

WE ALL SHARE THE EARTH'S WEALTH...
AND THE FAIREST WAY TO SHARE IT
IS THROUGH JUST TAXATION

It is frequently regarded as extremely clever to avoid payment of tax. Yet that is truly *antisocial;* it is a form of opting-out of civilization; it is unfair!

Positively, taxation gives a national economy the means to invest in all activities that lift up the quality of people's lives - industry, health, education, transport and culture.

PARTNERSHIP

WHETHER it be cans of beans or jumbo-jet aircraft, goods and services in our modern economy are produced through the *partnership of* a large number of working people. So, Will Hutton emphasises the need for trust and cooperation in production, organisation and financing of industry and commerce. He cites the success of much industry in Germany, achieved through mutual commitment by capital and labour to the prosperity of both company and personnel.

The success-story of Japanese industry for many years also, Hutton shows, has the same basis:

> *'The firm is the core social unit of which individuals are members rather then simply workers. Unions are organised around the firm, which promises lifetime employment, social protection and a pension, and the firm expects commitment in return.' (The State We're In. pp.263,270)*

If our society-economy is to be free of the chronic anxiety and breakdown witnessed in recent history, this will only be attained by determined partnership and commitment, such as Jesus wrought when he called disciples to commit themselves to the mission of the kingdom of God, and sent them out to *'proclaim the kingdom of God and heal the sick'.* Theirs was a partnership of mutual service:

> *'When (on your mission) you enter a town', Jesus told them, 'eat what is set before you; heal the sick in it" (Luke 10.8).* *(See also p. 61).*

Here we have the pattern for a prosperous economy -

commitment - partnership - mutual service.

THE NATION

IF a human society is to *ensure* that its economic needs are met -for food, transport or employment, for example- rather than being left to chance or charity, its members must commit themselves to *the making of laws and the keeping of them:* by so doing they are creating a NATION - or 'state'.

People committed to a national life are repudiating any notion they might have to disregard society or to affirm unfettered individualism: that is anarchy.

However, many people are disillusioned about national political life. Why? Partly because we are lazy and selfish, and partly because politicians have let their people down too often. Yet the general truth that we get out of life what we put in applies to politics. If we don't bother to vote in an election, we cannot complain if we have a poor government. If we take no interest and make no effort to involve ourselves in improving our children's education or our economy or standards of behaviour, for instance, what possibility of progress in learning or prosperity or good order in our nation will there be?

IT AIN'T WHAT YOU DO
IT'S THE WAY THAT YOU DO IT!

IF our national life is to be marked by fairness, honesty and vibrancy, such traits must be the fruit of an *enthusiastic commitment of each citizen.*

From government ministers to borough surveyors, from factory managers to office cleaners, from the milkman to the shop-assistant, there needs to be a determination to be just, true and keen in the carrying-out of our appointed tasks. Each of us needs to believe passionately in society: that our fellow-citizens are precious – as persons, customers, colleagues. Here again, Jesus is our exemplar: his intense spirit of love for the individual and for society *(Book Two)* can be ours.

Let us now see how the *nation* can help to *ensure* various areas of its citizens' needs.

CRIME

ONE of the prime and necessary functions of the nation-state is to deal with crime and the punishment and rehabilitation of offenders. A nation, directed by Christian, moral ways will have a distinctive and constructive policy.

PUNISHMENT

The Christian manner of punishment is guided by Jesus' way of non-retaliation: that is, punishment is not vengeance; 'an eye for an eye'. But it is the swift restraint of the offender, and imprisonment when advisable: all designed to *protect* the populace; to *emphasise* the wrong of his or her crime to the offender; and to *demonstrate the concern for the reform* of the offender by society and nation. The term of any imprisonment has to be measured by the gravity of the offence.

REHABILITATION OF THE OFFENDER

The mercy of God on imperfect people and our forgiveness of people who treat us badly (see *Part 1* of this *Book)* is our basic principle here. Jesus set out his policy:

> *'I have come to seek and save what is lost.' (Luke 19.10).*
>
> *'First take the plank out of your own eye, and then you will see clearly*

to take the speck out of your brother's.' (Matthew 7.5).
'Let whichever of you is free from sin throw the first stone...' (John 8.7).

A 16th century follower of Jesus, John Bradford, on seeing some criminals being led to execution, exclaimed: '...*but by the grace of God there goes John Bradford.'*

We must indeed 'put ourselves into the other person's shoes' and as surely as a good doctor must find the root-cause of a disease, because he wants to cure his patient, so we must seek out the motive of an offender if we are to stop him/her doing wrong again, and also to save his soul.

However, the Christian desire to understand the wrongdoer is in marked contrast to a prevalent attitude, spoken of by Jimmy Boyle: the stance of many adults and policemen toward him as a 'bad boy' at school was damning:

'None of them ever made me feel that they wanted me to be any different to how I was.' (A Sense of Freedom).

Truly the root-cause of so much crime reaches down to the early years of life. The 'Moors Murderer', Ian Brady, was abandoned as an infant by his father and mother in turn. He lived with an aunt and other relatives who treated him more as a toy than a child. He was given his own way and bad behaviour went unchecked. Thus the seeds of later wantonness were sown as he 'played' cruelly with children's lives.

Darren (not his real name) an out-of-control 15-year-old who has robbed, killed cats, rats and rabbits for fun, and set fire to his school, is being treated at the 'Youth At Risk' project at Brathay Hall in the English Lake District. It has been discovered that he has been abused since childhood - beaten and locked in a cupboard for hours. He has visited on others the violence done to him.

Once we realise the roots of criminality, we may use the appropriate means to cure the offender:

help him/her to come to terms with the past and the anger;
give courage when possible to apologise to the victim;
replace or repair spoiled property.

This is the programme of 'tough love' used at Brathay Hall.

CRIME PREVENTION

Though 'prevention is better than cure', the curing of the criminal mind (see above) is the surest way of crime-prevention ! Prevention will also be aided by urging every citizen to make it harder to commit crime: we can block off temptation by securing our homes, businesses and property, and avoiding ostentation.

'THE GOOSE THAT LAYS THE GOLDEN EGG'

THE south-west wind does not have to be stopped by British Customs & Excise, asking, *'Anything to declare?'* Rain-bearing clouds have not to be checked-in by H.M. Coastguard. Britannia does not rule the beneficial Gulf Stream. Our total environment is the whole Earth - and the atmosphere around it. However, 'on the ground' our environment is our country-nation, and the nation-state has a corresponding responsibility to deal with environmental issues within its borders. The issues are complicated, and here we shall only set out broad principles.

We can still in this modern world agree with the ancient Hebrews' belief in God's purpose and provision of our surroundings *(Psalm 104.13-15):*

> *'FROM your dwelling you water the hills;*
> *the earth is enriched by your provision.*
> *You make grass growjor the cattle and plants for the use of mortals,*
> *producing grain from the earth, food to sustain their strength,*
> *wine to gladden the hearts of the people,*
> *and oil to make their faces shine.'*

Yet we must take into account the greatly increased population in the last 2 to 3000 years, and the enlarged 'appetite' of modern industry for raw materials - from metals to plant-products. Realising this, our basic policy must be 'not to kill the goose that lays the golden egg'. That 'goose' is truly colossal and includes reserves of oil, plankton and forests and a myriad species of plants and animals, each contributing to the very basis of our bodily life with its needs such as proteins and vitamins.

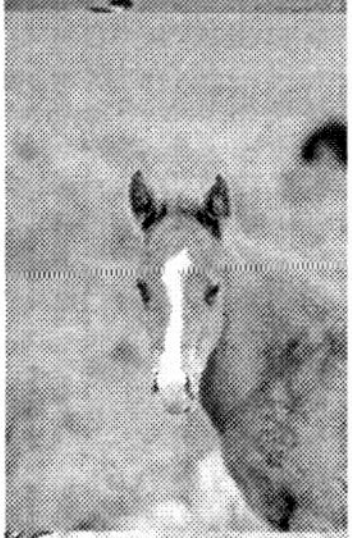

It is urgent then that we as a nation take steps to conserve our resources:

- *halt the unsustainable depletion of minerals and fuels for industry - by the use of alternative materials and sources of energy. These may include renewable means*

such as solar, wave and wind power;

- *preserve the stock of plant life including forests (140,000 miles of hedgerows were lost between 1945 and 1989);*

- *take steps to halt the extinction of animal species (loss of hedgerows by the assault of pesticide and plough has starved mammals and birds such as the tree-sparrow - down 89%, and song-thrush - down 73%* in 25 *years). Skylarks, on the contrary, many lost through winter-sowing, are reviving where farmers have reverted to sowing in spring;*
- *reduce the number of private-car journeys, increase use of public transport, and use alternative vehicle-fuels such as gas and electricity.*

If all these goals are to be achieved, the role of the nation-state is vital. It will listen to the concerns of business, agriculture and ecologists, and then enact necessary legislation.

WE have enjoyed our environment,
what shall we leave to our offspring ?

EDUCATION

'EDUCATION is life,
looked at from the point of
learning to live that life.'

This was said at a conference many years ago. The definition indicates the importance and comprehensiveness of education to a nation's citizens. The purpose of every school and college, and of all media, from literature to television, is to help people to live well in body, mind and soul. Hence, a nation's education system should aim at being *broad.* Whilst an individual scholar may have a bias to science or art, and may have a special fascination for some exotic subject, the preparation for life calls for pupils to be given a 'broad sweep' of subjects:

- *'... basic sciences such as mathematics, physics, biology;*
- *subjects which open minds to the context of our lives in time (history) and space (geography);*
- *courses which stimulate the sense of life's beauty (painting and music);*
- *a study of language, our own and other people's;*

- *subjects that aid understanding of life's meaning and*
- *relationships such as poetry, biography, society, logic, philosophy and religious studies.*

The nation, in order to attain such a width of learning, should endorse completely the challenge of the United Nations' Universal Declaration of Human Rights (Article 26); *'Education shall be free, at least in the elementary and fundamental stages.'* We should go further and provide free education through to university level, although financial constraints may require the repayment of funds by graduates from their subsequent income perhaps over a period of 20 years. This arrangement will allow students to concentrate on their courses without financial distraction, and so be a priceless investment in the talent and knowledge of our citizens.

FREE-THOUGHT AND RELIGION

> *'EVERYONE has the right to freedom of thought, conscience and religion … and to manifest his religion or belief in teaching, practice, worship and observance.'*
> *(UN Universal Declaration of Human Rights, Article 18)*

As we read this Article, agreed by the UN in 1948, we can almost hear the chains of tyranny falling off the people. Fascist governments who had recently silenced critics, and persecuted and then exterminated millions of Jews and others for their beliefs and cultures had been defeated.

We might assume that 50 years later freedom of thought and tolerance of varied religions would be 'taken as read'. This is far from the case. Still, discrimination, verbal abuse, burning of books, desecration of places of worship, and communal violence occur in nations around the world. Much of the worst conflicts and genocide we are witnessing today is rooted in a vile mixture of power-seeking, nationalism and religious intolerance.

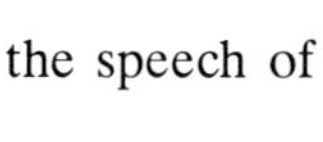

Freedom of thought and religion need to be established afresh, and reinforced by dialogue between thinkers with different philosophies, and between people of all faiths (Book *Four, Part I, pp. 150-152)* - just as Jesus the Jew did with the Samaritan woman *(John 4.8-30),* and the Roman Centurion *(Luke 7.1-10).*

WHO SHOULD RULE THE NATION?

THE outline of the answer to this question is found in the speech of President Abraham Lincoln, given at Gettysburg in 1863:

> *'…that this nation, under God, shall have a new birth of freedom; and that government of the people, by the people, and for the people, shall not perish from the earth.'*

Firstly, government *'of the people'.* A people/nation needs *government,* as the importance of taxation showed (see above). Each nation must have one *government* for one *people:* one body of law, one set of rules applied uniformly to all the nation. Lincoln aptly quoted Jesus in this context: *'A kingdom divided against itself cannot stand' (Mark 3.24),* and applied it to the United States of his time: *'I believe this government cannot endure permanently, half slave and half free'.* The folly and tragedy of people with divided allegiance is seen most starkly in Northern Ireland: an object lesson for every nation! And what about Palestine/Israel?

Secondly, rule must be *'by the people'.* Such rule is properly known as *democracy (Greek, 'people rule').* The basis is in Jesus' teaching and example, whereby he demonstrated the worth of each human being to God. (Book *Two, Part 1).* Further, Jesus spoke against *'lording it over'* people, and against hierarchies. *(Book Two, Part 2).* All citizens are equal, and are called to serve one another. Also *'government by the people'* is made more real when, whilst the one central rule is recognised in all the nation, much decision-making is devolved to regions, counties, districts and parishes. Thus, many people can share responsibility for the well-being of their fellow citizens. The equal status of each person also implies each one's right to vote by secret ballot for the election of each area of government from nation to parish.

Thirdly, government is *'for the people'.* This uncannily echoes the strong assertion of the Hebrew prophets:

> *'Woe betide Israel's shepherds (leaders)*
> *who care only for themselves!*
> *Should not the shepherd care for the flock?'*
> *(Ezekiel 34.2)*

The regime of a nation is not for the sake of the prosperity of the regime, but for the well-being of the people. So, the greatest people of the nation - for Jesus - are not those who amass wealth and power for themselves, but those who serve the needs of others.

We may apply to a nation's government this commentary on Jesus' teaching about greatness - by William Barclay:

> *The world may assess a man's greatness by the number of people he controls and who are at his beck and call; . . or by the number of committees of which he is a member; or by the size of his bank-balance . .; but in the assessment of Jesus Christ these things are irrelevant. His assessment is quite simply- how many people have you helped ?' (Gospel according to Matthew, Vol. 2, p. 257)*

THE PROPER MEASUREMENT OF A GREAT NATIONAL GOVERNMENT IS:
HOW MANY PEOPLE HAS IT HELPED ?

Society - Economy - Nation

A pictorial overview

SOCIETY is people needing people for companionship and service - laying down streets, pavements and building shops and Churches...

playing together from childhood to seniority...

Vulnerable people - orphans and handicapped - need others to care for them.

Some members of society raise money to provide care for those in need...

People needing people - that is the worth of society.

THE ECONOMY depends on the resources of the earth and the labour of human beings on land and sea.

The modern industrial world has produced large communities requiring housing and necessary financial services.

ALL our economy is meant to provide each citizen with daily bread of which there is enough for everyone's need...

but not for everyone's greed!

ALL humankind live in countries possessing natural resources that need to be preserved and managed.

This is a key function of the Nation.

A civilized Nation consists of people communicating with people.

Communication is aided by education at school and, maybe University

All concerns of the Nation, whether environment, crime, education or health are best ordered by the people electing local or national councils. Government 'by the people and for the people'.

MAKING SENSE OF LIFE - BOOK THREE

GOD AND THE MORAL WORLD

Part Four

One God, One World, One Human Race

The world feeds the World

The World... at war and at peace

United Nations... agency of harmony

'THE WORLD'S MINE OYSTER'

SO said Pistol in Shakespeare's *'Merry Wives of Windsor'* And as a pearl can be extracted from an oyster, so the Earth -the whole Earth- is the place from which you and I and every human being can extract profit and benefit for our lives.

Human beings are not trees, planted in one place and unable to move anywhere else on Earth. We have legs to walk, north, south, east or west; we have eyes to look around to every horizon; we have minds to muse on what might be over the hill!

However, in spite of this fact, we can choose to ignore the great, big world- like the rhymer in Kipling's *'The Five Nations'*:

'God gives men all the earth to love, but since man's heart is small,
ordains for each one spot shall prove beloved over all.
Each to his choice, and I rejoice the lot has fallen to me in a fair
ground - in a fair ground - yea Sussex by the sea!'

A large proportion of people are 'rooted' mentally and spiritually, if not actually, to one piece of ground. These folk could present little problem in global and human relations until of course 'foreigners' try to intrude on their plot, even for such innocent reasons as trade or tourism. Then, through ignorance of fellow-inhabitants of the wider world they become the 'patriots' of a tribal or national war-machinc, rcady to fight all 'comers'. We call this *xenophobia!* But our global problems really begin with that proportion of people who do regard the world as 'mine oyster'. Such people in the main don't intend to make trouble; they just do what comes naturally to being human: they walk; they wish to 'see the world'; they want to meet, transact and sometimes settle down with other folk. Such are like the sea-rover of John Masefield's poem:

'I must down to the seas again, to the lonely sea and the sky,
And all I ask is a tall ship and a star to steer her by..
I must down to the seas again, for the call of the running tide
Is a wild call and a clear call that may not be denied.'

And Kipling's British soldier has 'itchy feet':

'By the old Moulmein Pagoda, lookin' eastward to the sea,
There's a Burma girl a-settin', and I know she thinks o' me;
For the wind is in the palm-trees, an' the temple-bells they say:
"Come you back, you British soldier; come you back to Mandalay!"'

Yet the movement and meeting of people around the Earth originates largely from even more 'down-to-earth' reasons than 'roving'. What those who are mentally 'rooted' to one spot try to shut out of their mind is the *99% necessity* for people to move and to meet others. Life's survival, let alone progress , demands movement, and this has never been more so than at the beginning of the 3rd Millennium - 'economic migrants', asylum-seekers, and all!

ONE of my favourite places is the south end of Southend Pier. There you can see the meaning of '*one Earth, one human race'*.

You can watch the ships sailing in and out of the Thames estuary: oil-tankers from the Middle East; freighters bringing lamb from New Zealand, oranges from Israel, motor cars from Spain; other cargo-vessels are exporting from Britain machinery, textiles, aircraft-engines, glassware, pottery, paper... to all over the world.

Then also among the freighters are the cruise-ships, replete with folk who want to see exotic lands across the sea.

Indeed the lives of most of us on this Earth would be poverty-stricken if we did not move and meet. Further, by so doing many thousands of people can earn their living in our factories and farms, and in our markets and transport. We only have to walk along the nearest high-street or into our local supermarket, and take the trouble to look carefully at the inscription on the bottom of the plate and see MADE IN CHINA, or read the label on the packet: PRODUCE OF ITALY. To understand this:

> *the real world we live in is bigger than my village or town or nation; it is the whole Earth!*

GOD'S PURPOSE FOR THE ONE HUMAN RACE

WE set out the moral way of life - under God - of our *society-economy-nation* - in *Part 3.* The One God has the same purpose for every citizen of every nation in the one Earth, namely:

> *to learn how to live together in righteousness and harmony.*

This purpose is admirably expressed in the second command of Jesus: *'You shall love your neighbour as yourself' (Mark 12.31)* - and then set out clearly in Article 1 of the United Nations' *Universal Declaration of Human Rights (1948)*:

'All human beings are born free and equal in dignity and rights. They are endowed with reason and conscience and should act towards one another in a spirit of brotherhood.'

BEGINNING THE THIRD MILLENNIUM - WHERE HAS THE 'SPIRIT OF BROTHERHOOD' GONE?

ARE people 'free and equal' in your nation? I hope so! Perhaps 'brotherhood' is alive and well around you. I trust it is! But sadly many millions of people in the world would 'give the earth' to feel free and safe. We could give an 'A-to-Z' list of nations presently deprived of freedom from want or fear from Afghanistan, Algeria and Angola, through Burma, Colombia, Iraq, Liberia, Rwanda, Tibet to Yugoslavia.

Erskine Childers captured the true world situation at the end of the 20th century in the Introduction to his book, 'Challenges to the UN' (1994):

'When the Cold war seemed to end, there was a burst of euphoria across the northern part of the world, that now at last there would be an 'era of peace'... In the event... we are in an era of constantly expanding eruptions of civil collapse, violence and mass human misery to which no culture or region is immune.'

(Those words echo now in the new century as violence occurs in places like the Middle East, Indonesia and Zimbabwe, and more persecuted people seek asylum in European countries.)

The assessment was endorsed by Lady Thatcher in a speech at Fulton, USA in 1996:

'When Soviet power broke down, so did the control it exercised, however fitfully and irresponsibly, over rogue states. (This) also aggravated the single most awesome threat of modern times: the proliferation of weapons of mass destruction. These weapons... are today acquired by... countries such as Iraq, Iran, Libya and Syria... Of the nations that have or are acquiring such weapons, many are led by megalomaniacs and strongmen of proven inhumanity or by weak, unstable or illegitimate governments... That means the west must install effective ballistic missile defences which would protect us... and enable us to retaliate.'

Much of Lady Thatcher's analysis is accurate and her call for vigilance and capable defence is worldly-wise. However, her speech contains, apart from the deployment of weapons, no suggestion about how the dangers may positively be dealt with; no mention of the good offices of the United Nations. Her realism is needed, but the best way to be rid of enemies is to turn them into friends; the building of better international relations is urgently required.

WORKING OUT GOD'S GLOBAL PURPOSE

LET us try then to assemble positive activities in the cause of the freedom, justice and peace for all the world's people.

We cannot hope to achieve this goal unless we are aware of the colossal nature of the task.

Like Heracles in the Greek story we are faced with Hydra, the many headed monster: we cannot succeed if we tackle only one of the many causes of strife. Just as the forces of democracy were faced by hostile powers on several fronts in the 2nd World War and fought them all at the same time, such is the many-sided endeavour needed to win the salvation of humankind around the world from war, killing and destruction.

What are the Causes of Strife?

- DIVISION - leading to alienation, hostility, ignorance and prejudice
- DESIRE for POWER and WEALTH - leading to injustice and oppression
- FEAR - leading to defence and the arms-race

Let us expand on these headings, and examine how to deal with them.

DIVISION

'Jews have no dealings with Samaritans', John's Gospel (4.9) tells us. Almost 2000 years later many Jews and Arabs are hostile to one another. Such disunity occurs repeatedly. A native of Nigeria recently asserted that her country had many languages, and even more tribes, who *'have nothing in common'.* Sri Lanka is bitterly divided between Sinhalese and Tamils, who have slaughtered each other for many years. Hutu and Tutsi peoples in central Africa have indulged in mutual genocide. The relatively small island of Cyprus is deeply cleft between Greeks and Turks. The huge Indian subcontinent is fissured by Hindu India and Muslim Pakistan and Bangladesh. Irishmen, Nationalists and Unionists, trade insults and guns. The list is much longer!

The last-mentioned instance perhaps gives us an insight into this cause of strife. Tragically the political division between Nationalists and Unionists prevailingly corresponds to the religious persuasions of both sides: Catholic and Protestant. The most fanatical devotees of each side illustrate the basic principle referred to in *Part 1:*

'Believing in God's punishment in Hell can lead... to the perpetuation of hatred and feuds.'

The Protestant leader, the Rev. Ian Paisley, railed against the Roman Catholics in the 1950s: *'I have hated God's enemies with a perfect hate.' (Liam de Paor: 'Divided Ulster' p.152).* His religious opponents are utterly 'black' and damned: they are the *'forces of popery and the scarlet whore' (De Paor op. cit. p.152)* Paisley described opponents in Rome in 1996 as *'blaspheming, cursing, spitting Roman scum'. ('Ulster: The Sunday Times Insight Team' p.42).* The 'enemy' is so condemned by God that they lose their divinely-created human image: *'any shortage of houses and jobs (in N. Ireland) is all the fault of the Papists, since, "... these people breed like rabbits and multiply like vermin".' (Paisley's 'Protestant Telegraph' quoted in 'Ulster', op. cit. p.149).* Belief in violent punishment in 'Hell' is common to much Roman Catholic and Protestant teaching in Ireland.

Thus people *act out their belief*. Irish paramilitaries carry out 'punishment-beatings' and knee-capping. Elsewhere, some Hutus killed the 'cockroaches' - Tutsis. The massacre of the enemies' children is justified: *'When you kill rats, you don't spare babies.'* Genocide of those who had previously massacred is to be celebrated because *'God rewards the just.' (T.V. Documentary)* Holding such beliefs, there is little hope of understanding, tolerance or compromise, and division only deepens: there can be 'no surrender' to God's enemies, no meeting of minds, no power-sharing, and NO MERCY. This is the root of our worst conflicts.

WHAT IS THE ANSWER TO DIVISION?

AS a powerful virus can only be overcome by a more potent antibiotic, so division and strife can only be eliminated by a stronger adversary. Such is the ONE GOD OF LOVE. Jesus received God's love for the Samaritans whom his fellow-Jews despised, but who to him were beloved 'neighbours'. Neighbourly love has no limit on God's ONE EARTH. Every human being is more than a fellow-traveller or a 'cousin'. She is my *sister*; he is my *brother*: my *kith and kin*; God's *child*. Like me!

This truth is voiced by Fred Dallas in his 20th century folk-song:

'I belong to a family, the biggest on earth,
a thousand every day are coming to birth...
From the North Pole ice to the snow at the other
there isn't a man I wouldn't call my brother.'

Let us see an example of this *' brotherhood'* and *unity-building* power.

A group of people in the Canterbury district of England formed an Association during the 'Cold War' between 'East' and 'West' in 1985 in order to help to break down the division. Their aim was to link Canterbury with a town in the Soviet Union and another in the USA Five years of persistent probing resulted in contacts between Canterbury, Vladimir (Russia) and Bloomington, Illinois. Visits and friendships developed, and to this day (2003) cooperation among the towns involves aspects of life such as culture, education, sport, police-work and religion.

Glimpses of Unity-Building

Top left: First delegation from Vladimir share lunch. (L-R: Councillor Petrenko, The Author, Dr. Yesavlov, Kathleen Hill, V. Kuzin - Mayor of Vladimir).
Top right: Visitors quiz farmer about cattle-rearing.
Bottom left: Visit to Canterbury of Vladimir Musatov, Deputy Mayor of Vladimir (L-R, Dr David Ormrod, The Author, V. Musatov).
Bottom left: British visiors received in the office of Vladimir City Soviet(standing - Betty Collins, interpreting, with The Author speaking in Russian!).
Centre: Celebratory cake at reception for Russian Delegation at Whitstable, Kent.

Kipling wrote in 1892: *'Oh, East is East, and West is West, and never the twain shall meet..'* That seemed to prevail in 1985: Russians and British were strangers, aliens, especially 'in the mind'. But the spirit of unity and love changed all that for those who travelled to each other's country - like a group of clergymen, for example, from the Canterbury Diocese; seven Anglicans and two United Reformed Church Ministers (and some wives) - who went to Vladimir as guests of the Russian Orthodox Church in 1990. One evening the group, along with priests visited a tavern in the countryside. After the meal a party of Russian sportsmen from Kostroma , up North on the Volga, began to sing folk-songs. When they had finished they called on us to sing for them - and were regaled with *'On Ilkla Moor baht hat' and 'Sospan fach'* - to their obvious delight!

People living 1000s of miles apart found themselves with so much in common - enjoying company, humour and singing, and parting was 'such sweet sorrow'!

The Canterbury Three Towns Association practice of unity and love needs to be repeated all over the world. Moreover, the Author's travels in Russia, Germany, France, Belgium and Ireland reveals people's prevailing goodwill and love of peace. More contact is needed to 'harness' the goodwill, and this can be made to happen in varied ways.

TWINNING OF TOWNS. This movement which has developed since the hostilities of 1939-45 has made a contribution to the healing of the 'enemy' nations of Europe. Yet the signs of 'backsliding' alienation are with us today, calling for perseverance and fresh vigour in response, and an extension of 'twinning' from Europe to the wider Earth - as we shall explain.

CULTURAL EXCHANGES. Russians and British singing together is but one instance of all that humankind can share. Many cultural activities can help to unite folk, from ballet to basketball, snooker to symphony orchestras, skiing to stamp-collecting.

INTER-FAITH MEETINGS. If people's religious faith perversely causes some of the deepest and cruellest conflicts - as recently in the Middle East, the Balkans, Chechnya, Nigeria and Indonesia - then obviously devotees of various faiths need to meet, firstly to try to understand one another, and secondly to replace isolation and hatred by cooperation and love. So, a Christian Church in Britain could be 'twinned' with a Mosque in Libya, or a Synagogue in France with a Sikh Gurdwara in India. (See further in *Book Four, Part 1, pp. 150-152).* This could open minds and hearts and construct a reconciled and peaceful world.

'PEOPLE-MEETING AGENCY'. If the above activities are desirable, they require a major effort. The UN should set up such an 'agency' to coordinate and finance 'twinnings' and exchanges. Major funds and personnel could be transferred from the arms budget and the military, which would truly be a 'peace-dividend'! Again, 'enemies' would be transformed into friends!

DESIRE FOR POWER AND WEALTH

THIS cause of conflict reaches way back into history. Pastoral societies more than 3000 years ago were involved, as the Hebrew Book of Genesis tells:

'Since Lot, who was travelling with Abram, also possessed sheep and cattle and tents, the land could not support them while they were together. They had so much livestock that they could not settle in the same district, and quarrels arose between Abram's herdsmen and Lot's.' (13.5-7)

'Little local difficulties' such as that escalated with time to imperial wars, as great powers like those in Babylonia and Egypt sought to extend their wealth and influence. So, from the empire-building of Persia, Greece and Rome in ancient times to that of modern Britain, France, Germany and Japan wars have plagued humankind. The patriotic song of 1902 put into words the ambition of the imperialists, in this case of Britain:

'Land of hope and glory, mother of the free..
Wider still and wider shall thy bounds be set;
God who made thee mighty, make thee mightier yet!'

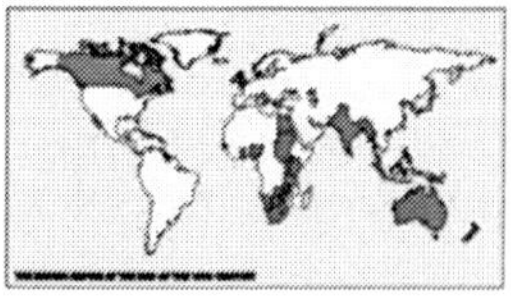

Similar was the ambition of Hitler's Germany in the 1930s, captured in this slogan:

'Heute gehort uns Deutschland - morgen die ganze Welt!'
('Today Germany belongs to us - tomorrow the whole world.')

Germany, having lost its overseas empire after 1918, and made weak by defeat in the 1st World War, aimed to make the country a great power again, and to expand its area to provide more living-space and food for the growing nation. This aspiration led to the take-over of Austria and Czechoslovakia and the invasion of Poland. So the war beginning in 1939 was provoked by desire for wealth and power.

SHARING WEALTH AND POWER

IF it is the desire for wealth and power that leads to injustice and oppression - and ultimately to war - then it is the *sharing* of wealth and power that leads to fairness and respect for others in each nation and between all nations, resulting in peace. We shall try to show how this goal may be reached when we deal with the United Nations, federalism and world government later.

FEAR

A falconer in his wisdom wears a glove as a defence, should the bird of prey chance to attack his hand. Likewise, if we have any cause to fear a hostile tribe or an ambitious empire, our reaction is to build up armaments to deter or defend.

Long ago the Roman military writer, Vegetius, wrote, *'Let him who desires peace, prepare for war.'*

Sometimes this policy works: possibly the possession of nuclear arsenals by 'East' and 'West' in recent decades is an example. But preparing for war is not a cast-iron guarantee of keeping the peace. Preparation can easily provoke an 'arms race' and set off war as one side hopes to strike the 'killer- punch' first. We can demonstrate this by citing two cases: the preparations for war by the great powers before 1914; and the build-up of armaments by the Arab nations and Israel prior to war in 1967.

CASE 1 THE GREAT WAR, 1914-18

Pre 1914

SOLDIERS		BATTLESHIPS	
GERMANY	*2.2 millions*	*BRITAIN*	*64*
RUSSIA	*1.4 million*	*GERMANY*	*40*
FRANCE	*1.25 million*	*FRANCE*	*28*

SUCH POWER did not prevent a war that lasted over 4 years and caused more than 10 million soldiers to perish.

CASE 2 ARAB-ISRAELI SIX-DAY WAR, 1967

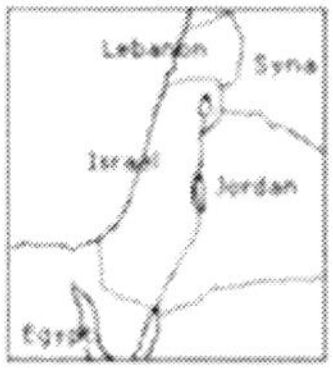

BOTH SIDES built up strong armies and airforces. The ARAB states of Syria, Jordan and Lebanon massed troops along the borders of ISRAEL in 1967, then joined forces with Egypt which was ready to attack Israel. The Israelis were surrounded, but decided that the best policy was to ATTACK FIRST, rather than to sit around awaiting to be destroyed.

ISRAEL'S powerful airforce bombed and destroyed most of Egypt's warplanes on the ground and their army advanced on all fronts to win the war in six days!

YET nearly forty years later hostility between Arabs and Israelis still often leads to bloodshed!

Indeed, mutual suspicion, hostility and the build-up of forces are a very shaky foundation for peace. They also impoverish nations and brutalise whole generations. This has been the case in Iraq in recent decades, and in the year 2000 Zimbabwe was short of fuel for its civilian transport because it was driving its military vehicles in war in Congo!

SWORDS INTO PLOUGHSHARES

WE are about to argue for *world-wide disarmament* as a condition for global peace. Yet we must remind ourselves of the *'Hydra'* we are facing: disarmament must be joined with our other efforts for peace-building, that is, unity and love, people-meeting and wealth- and power-sharing. This is a vast and revolutionary operation, which only a vigorous - and re-formed - *United Nations* can perform.

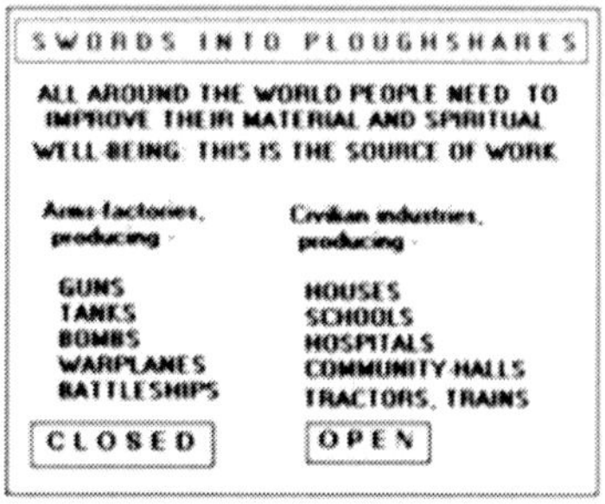

Returning to the replacement of the arms-industry itself, this is as difficult as turning around a 100,000 tons oil-tanker. We are dealing with a megabusiness.

The biggest arms-seller, the USA, trades $10 billions-worth each year, and is closely followed by Russia. France and Britain rank as 3rd and 4th in arms sales, Britain earning £5 billion from exports in 1995, 20% of the world market in cash terms. Should the British arms industry close its factories, 350, 000 workers would be made redundant. Moreover the orders for guns, tanks and warplanes would go straight to the USA, Russia or France, or even to Spain or Egypt.

ONE NATION ACTING ALONE WILL NOT STOP THE FLOOD OF ARMAMENTS TO THE WORLD.
NO! ALL NATIONS MUST ACT TOGETHER!

It is equally imperative that there be put in place a universal plan for the *conversion* of arms factories to constructive manufacture, thus creating fresh employment for the redundant workers. What other work would be available? *(See chart above).*

People Meeting People
Canterbury (UK) < > Vladimir (Russia) < > Bloomington (USA)

Further, should a UN 'People Meeting Agency' be formed, this would require an 'army' of organisers and more personnel employed in the increased movement of people by land, sea and air, and their service in hotels, hostels and restaurants.

Here we have an alternative, constructive global industry, which can only be built up through the partnership of *ALL* nations: a powerful argument for a robust *UNITED NATIONS!*

THE UNITED NATIONS, FEDERALISM AND WORLD GOVERNMENT

'AN earth-shattering event'! Surely the 2nd World War came as near as ever to being just that! Destructive forces were unleashed on an unprecedented scale. Millions of people were killed and left grieving kin.

The aggressive powers were only defeated by many nations *united* in resolve and commitment to ridding humankind of violent racism and injustice. These nations formed the UNITED NATIONS ORGANISATION in 1945, in the words of its *CHARTER:*

'... to save succeeding generations from the scourge of war, which twice in our lifetime has brought untold sorrow to mankind'

Unfortunately the nations of the world at the beginning of the 21st century are too much like an alcoholic, who after a particularly bad hangover vows he will 'never touch a drop of the drink again' - only to do that very thing a few hours later! So, the 50 and more years since 1945 have seen over 120 wars, some big some small, even though the UN has tried, and sometimes succeeded, in prevention. Simultaneously the UN has striven to improve living-standards through its agencies such as the Food & Agriculture Organisation, the World Health Organisation and the International Children's Fund, but has seen many projects undermined by unjust national regimes and profiteering international business. Unruly and greedy people around the world have thwarted the UN.

Most importantly, the UN has been compromised and crippled by a serious fault in the very design of its organisation, namely, the existence and use of the *VETO,* possessed by the five permanent members: USA, Soviet Union/Russia, China, Britain and France. Their veto has been used from time to time to serve their national interest and block UN decisions.

This is a denial of the unity of all the nations, because, however the rest of the nations vote, if one of the 'Five' disagrees, then the majority's vote is discounted. Is there then any wonder that many nations are 'cool' toward the UN, and disregard its rulings or do not 'pull their weight' either in contributing finance or personnel to its operations - on the principle, 'no taxation without representation'?

Moreover, recently the 'Five' have developed an offhand attitude to the UN. The USA and UK for example lead NATO's defiance of the UN in attacking Serbia; and Russia refused the UN Secretary-General's plea for a cessation of the cruel bombardment of Chechnya. These acts by the 'leading powers' are an even worse example to the nations of the world. They display self- and national-interest and immaturity that should have no place in an organisation that is serious about achieving the unity and harmony of humankind.

So, at the beginning of the 3rd Millennium the UN faces a deep crisis of credibility. It is widely seen to be impotent to prevent serious conflict and deadly war - its prime reason for existence.

WHAT CAN BE DONE?

Should the UN be scrapped?

Or, Can it be reconstructed?

BUILDING A REFORMED UNITED NATIONS

A REFORMED UNITED NATIONS has first to dismantle the old organisation, based upon national self-interest. Then, a new structure must be built on a firmer foundation.

What is this foundation?

THE foundation of a reformed UNITED NATIONS is our acceptance of the TWO REALITIES OF OUR LIFE ON EARTH, namely

- THE INDIVIDUAL HUMAN BEING'S SACRED RIGHT TO LIVE IN BODY, MIND AND SOUL
- *OUR COMMITMENT TO SHARE IN THE WORLD-WIDE COMMUNITY.*

There are obvious tensions between the individual and the community, yet life's challenge is to care both for the individual *and* the community. This is truly the case with the UN, because its purpose is to promote the well-being of people the world over, as aptly expressed in the U.N's *Universal Declaration of Human Rights, Article 1:*

> *'ALL human beings are born free and equal in dignity and rights.*
> *They are endowed with reason and conscience*
> *and should act towards one another in a spirit of brotherhood.'*

UPON this foundation the reformed UNITED NATIONS will be built!

THE REBUILT UNITED NATIONS

REPRESENTATIVE OF EVERY HUMAN BEING

The new UN should fairly represent every human being (not the nations with the greatest wealth or force). Membership of its councils will be based on nations, but according to their populations, thus:

GENERAL ASSEMBLY - One member for every 100 millions.

Every nation with 50 millions or less will have one member: between 50 and 100 millions - 2 members. Larger nations have an extra member for every 100 millions. TOTAL MEMBERSHIP - 238. Decisions by 66% majority.

SECURITY COUNCIL - One member for each nation with over 50 millions population. 5 members from nations with over 25 million population (by rota for 4-year periods). 5 members from all other nations (by rota for 3-year periods).

One member (by rota) representing nations of Australasia. TOTAL MEMBERSHIP - 34

Decisions by 60% majority. The largest - permanent - members are: CHINA, INDIA, USA, INDONESIA, BRAZIL, RUSSIA, JAPAN, PAKISTAN, BANGLADESH, MEXICO, NIGERIA, GERMANY, VIETNAM, PHILIPPINES, ETHIOPIA, UK, ITALY, TURKEY, FRANCE, EGYPT, THAILAND, IRAN & UKRAINE.

COMMITMENT TO HUMAN RIGHTS

The nations shall decide together a code of human rights *(see present 'code' appended to this Part)*, and commit themselves to the publishing and observance of them.

COMMITMENT TO UNITY & DISCIPLINE

A nation's membership of the UN will entail a commitment to the world-wide community, to common action, and to abide by the democratically- made decisions of its councils.

(That is, when violations of international relations or internal human rights are adjudicated by the UN, each member-nation commits itself to abide by the council's decision: no nation possesses a veto.)

This is *'Federalism'. *See note below.*

INCORPORATION OF EXISTING AGENCIES

Whilst the structure of 'superpower' domination is dismantled, UN Agencies such as the World Health Organisation, UNESCO and Relief & Works would be 'built in' to the new UN

MULTILATERAL DISARMAMENT

All nations will commit themselves to exclusively peaceful means of settling both international and internal disputes, and rid themselves of armaments, except for defence against criminals.

The arms industry will convert to construction, and military personnel to civilian occupations.

RECONCILIATION OF RELIGIONS

As religious ignorance and intolerance are igniting conflicts around the world, the UN will facilitate the dialogue, reconciliation and collaboration of the world's faiths in the cause of harmony.

FEDERALISM & WORLD GOVERNMENT

PEOPLE can only live in peace when they *commit* themselves to one common law. Another word for 'commit' is 'covenant', an ancient concept used by the Israelites and by Jesus, translated in Latin as *'fedus' (English: 'treaty')*. 'Federalism' is a freely-entered treaty and commitment, and is the relationship of unselfish, mature people and nations, who meet in councils to cooperate, make decisions by majority vote, and then abide by them - as set out above: *'Commitment to Unity'*.

The rebuilt United Nations is thus a WORLD GOVERNMENT by treaty, and the *only* world-governing body. There must be no other alliances, such as NATO, acting as power-blocks to menace and divide the unity of humankind.

However, so many conflicts are *regional* - as with India and Pakistan, Ethiopia and Eritrea, Britain and Ireland - and the UN is needed most in the regions. So, Reform of the UN should include the fostering of *REGIONAL PARTNERSHIPS,* worldwide, to replace rivalry with cooperation for the enrichment of every citizen of every nation. How would this *enrichment* be achieved?

- Each Region would set up departments to deal with *economic development, health, education, human rights, ethical business, the environment, inter-faith relations and culture.*
- An audit of needs in all these fields would be matched to available skills.
- The training of workers to fill vacancies would be carried out.
- Philosophical, political, cultural and religious understanding would be fostered.

Imagine, therefore, India and Pakistan or Palestine and Israel or Ireland and Britain taking part in such a regional group. How life for their citizens would be changed for the better!

SO, a rebuilt UNITED NATIONS may turn the concept of *ONE GOD-ONE EARTH-ONE HUMAN RACE* into a glorious reality, by bringing mutual respect, human maturity and responsibility, and harmony to this world, where poverty, oppression, division and war have for far too long brought sadness and despair to so many.

If such a transformation is to come about, it requires the effort of every citizen of every nation. Like a sports-team the UN is only as good as each team-member *plays*. So, you and I are called to 'play our hearts out' as we respect, care for and cooperate with our fellow-human beings in all the world.

Is this not the will of God, who put us all on this Earth together?

Thus we pray with hymn-writer, Fred Kaan:

'For the healing of the nations, Lord, we pray
with one accord;
for a just and equal sharing of the things that
earth affords.
To a life of love in action help us rise and
pledge our word.'
('Rejoice and Sing' 620)

THE WASTE OF WAR

'Waste of Muscle, waste of Brain,
Waste of Patience, waste of Pain,
Waste of Manhood, waste of Health,
Waste of Blood and waste of Tears,
Waste of youth's most precious years,
Waste of ways the saints have trod,
Waste of Glory, waste of God,
War! '

THE AUTHOR of these lines, Studdert Kennedy, as a Chaplain in France in the First World War, saw the carnage that wasted the lives of millions of young men.

POISON GAS, first used in battle in France in 1915, only added to the gruesome weaponry 'successfully' deployed in warfare century after century.

JOSEPH SHEPHERD, the author's uncle, killed in the Battle of the Somme, on its last day, 18 November 1916.

SO that such men may not have died in vain,
we dedicate ourselves to work for peace.

THE UNIVERSAL DECLARATION OF HUMAN RIGHTS (1948)

A Summary Version

ARTICLE 1 ***EQUALITY***

All human beings are born free with the same rights.

ARTICLE 2

These rights apply to everyone whatever their colour, gender, religion or any other factor which might make them different from other people.

ARTICLE 3 ***FREEDOM***

Everyone has the right to life, and to live in freedom and safe from harm.

ARTICLE 4

No one shall be made a slave.

ARTICLE 5

No one shall be tortured or punished cruelly or treated in a degrading way.

ARTICLE 6 ***RECOURSE TO LAW***

Everyone counts as a full human person before the law.

ARTICLE 7

The law must be the same for everyone.

ARTICLE 8

Everyone living in a country has the right to seek help from a court if they do not get their legal rights.

ARTICLE 9

No-one shall be arrested or imprisoned or sent away from their country without proper reason.

ARTICLE 10

Everyone has the right to a fair and public hearing by an independent and impartial legal body.

ARTICLE 11

Everyone has the right to be treated as innocent until proved guilty by a court of law.

ARTICLE 12 ***PRIVACY***

Everyone has the right to privacy in their home, family and communication.

ARTICLE 13 ***MOVEMENT***

Everyone has the right to live where they like within their country, to move around it and to leave and return to it.

ARTICLE 14 ***REFUGE***

Everyone has the right to seek refuge in other countries from persecution in their own country.

ARTICLE 15 ***NATIONALITY***

Everyone has the right to belong to a country.

ARTICLE 16 ***MARRIAGE***

Men and women of full age... have the right to agree to marry each other and to found a family.

ARTICLE 17 ***PROPERTY***

Everyone has the right to own property

ARTICLE 18 ***THOUGHT & RELIGION***

Everyone has the right to freedom of thought, conscience and religion.

ARTICLE 19

Everyone has the right to hold an opinion and to express it.

ARTICLE 20

Everyone has the right to form associations and to gather together for peaceful purposes – and to choose not to take part in an association.

ARTICLE 21 ***DEMOCRACY***

Everyone has the right to participate in their government including the right to take part in choosing their country's government.

ARTICLE 22 ***SOCIAL SECURITY***

Everyone has the right to social security and to economic, social and cultural rights.

ARTICLE 23 ***EMPLOYMENT***

Everyone has the right to work in reasonable conditions and for a fair wage and to belong to a trade union.

ARTICLE 24 ***LEISURE***

Everyone has the right to rest and leisure and holiday from work.

ARTICLE 25 ***STANDARD OF LIVING***

Everyone has the right to an adequate standard of living.

ARTICLE 26 ***EDUCATION***

Everyone has the right to education.

ARTICLE 27 ***CULTURE***

Everyone has the right to participate freely in the cultural life of their community.

ARTICLE 28 ***WORLD ORDER***

Everyone is entitled to a social and international order in which these rights can come about.

ARTICLE 29 ***DUTY TO COMMUNITY***

Everyone has duties to their communities.

ARTICLE 30

Nothing in this Declaration may be interpreted as implying... any right to engage in any activity... aimed at the destruction of any of these rights

MAKING SENSE OF LIFE - BOOK FOUR

THE CHURCH AND THE FUTURE

Part One

The Church and Its Mission

THE CHURCH
Always Reforming and Uniting

-helping humankind to set sail across God's ocean to a world beyond our vision

THE CHURCH'S MISSSION

- in Belgium

- in Russia

- in Wales

'I THINK JESUS WAS A GOOD MAN, BUT I HAVE NO TIME FOR THE CHURCH!'

SUCH a common view would isolate Jesus from the Church. It may also raise such questions as: *'Did Jesus ever intend to found a Church?'* and, *'Does the Church have any place in the purpose of Jesus?'*

To answer these questions we must go back to the earliest records of Jesus' ministry: such as those we examined in *Book Two, Part 1,* that is the *'Sayings of Jesus Source "Q"'*. There we find no mention of the Church (Greek, *ekklesia*). Yet, another name is found to which the saying of Shakespeare's Juliet is apt: 'What's in a name? that which we call a rose, by any other name would smell as sweet...'

Jesus speaks a lot about the *'kingdom'*.

> *'God has chosen to give you the kingdom.' (Luke 12.32)*
> *'Blessed are you who are in need; the kingdom of God is yours.'*
> *'Proclaim the kingdom of God and heal the sick.'*
> *'When you pray, say, Father... your kingdom come.'*
> *'Set your minds on God's kingdom, and the rest will come to you as well.'*
> *(Luke 6.20; 9.2; 11.2; & 12.31)*

So, as Jesus' followers accept God's gift of fellowship and go out to aid the poor, heal the sick and receive hospitality; ask for God's way to prevail, and live by that way, they are establishing God's kingdom among people and are gathering an assembly of God's folk.

Disciples like Simon Peter are among this assembly, both in the Gospels and in the early letters of Paul, the latter written less than 25 years after Jesus' physical life. By this early time Jesus' community is called in Paul's letters, *ekklesia,* translated 'church'. Jesus, then, created a community called the 'kingdom of God', or, *'a rose by another name'* - the 'church'.

But more vital than the *name* is the *nature and purpose* of the CHURCH. This is the main concern of this *Part*.

JESUS' ORIGINAL VISION OF THE CHURCH

WHILST it is true that any community involving God and human beings will be a growing, developing society, it seems to this author to be important that we attempt to search for the original vision of Jesus, the 'spark' that set the blazing trail of the Church around the world, a trail which has progressed now for nearly 2000 years. If we fail to do this, we could well completely misunderstand the Church and its mission. So we must ask, *'What was Jesus' purpose for the Church?'*

Can we really discover this original vision? Well, we tried in *Book Two*, and we shall apply what we found out about Jesus' *'mission and message'*, his *'good news'*, to the Church's mission in our time.

THE CHURCH GOD'S LOVE-LETTER TO HUMANKIND

From GOD to the Church
'I want you to take a message of GOOD NEWS to everyone on Earth, many of whom are in deep trouble and can't believe that anyone cares- me included!'
My Child,
I want you to know that I love you. Like a father and mother I brought you into this world and I can never abandon you. Every hair of your head is precious to me!
I know all about you, the good and the bad. I want to encourage the good and help you by my mercy to admit and forsake the bad. Receive my good spirit that will lead you to goodness. Keep your eyes on Jesus: he has shown you the quality of love you need. Like you, he lived among many people who 'couldn't care less', but he never ceased to care all the way to the deadly cross.
So now, be happy in my mercy. Look forward in hope and care for each other. My love for you will never end. I will be with you wherever you go.
I am, YOUR MAKER and FRIEND

Does not this 'letter' indeed describe the Church's mission and message? Yet sadly, how much theology taught in the Church for much of its history - and today - has deviated from the original. The inconsistent 'God' referred to in *Book Two, Part 1, p. 49-50* has been preached. It has been put over that there is a limit to God's mercy, opening up the prospect of eternal punishment or separation from God - as for instance in the tract illustrated which was handed to the author in Norwich.

> *'It is God's will that all should come to repentance'... (but) those who remain unbelievers are classed as evil and will be raised... only to be cast into Hell where there is torment day and night for ever... Their's will be a living death. Please don't go that way.'*
>
> *('Scripture Truth')*

Can such teaching really be described as a *'gospel'/'good news'?* No!

The really good news is that Jesus shows us God's *unending* mercy and salvation. This is amply endorsed by the discoveries of modern science and the course of history, thus:

DISCOVERIES OF MODERN SCIENCE

The science of archaeology reveals both the immensely long history of the Earth - showing God's patience, and the intricate detail of creatures, great and small. This demonstrates God's concern for the tiniest of his 'handiwork'.

(See more in Book One, Part 2)

God has fed the birds of the air and the fish of the sea, age after age, as Jesus taught, and science shows. God's patient love never comes to an end.

THE COURSE OF HUMAN HISTORY

Much of human history has witnessed man's inhumanity to man, as in our picture of crusaders returning from Palestine, where they shared in the slaughter of thousands of their fellowmen - and in the name of 'God'! How near the end, do we feel, is God's patience?

The author of the *Book of Revelation,* writing about 1900 years ago, was sure that God would bring universal retribution on evildoers *'soon' (22.12)*, but 1000 years afterwards Crusaders and Saracens were still fighting - and God was still 'causing his sun to rise on good and bad alike', as Jesus noted.

Move on another 800 years and see God's forbearance remain. I travelled through the Pas de Calais and the valley of the Somme in France, where in 1916 hundreds of thousands of young men were mown down by one another's guns. My journey was in August 1970, and, where the battlefields had been, God's rain and sunshine -and man's ploughs - had produced fields of golden corn to give a new generation their daily bread. God, in his mercy, was still patiently showering his blessing on his offspring! Do not some words in the Jewish scriptures presage Jesus' *good news*. They express the essential teaching, preaching and living of the Church - *God's Love Letter (Lamentations of Jeremiah 3.22-3):*

> *'God's love is surely not exhausted, nor has his compassion failed;*
> *they are new every morning, so great is his constancy.'*

THE HOLY OF HOLIES

- Prayer -

The Church's Powerhouse

- *Where does he (Jesus) get it from?*
- *What is this wisdom he has been given?*
- *How does he perform such miracles?*
- *Is he not the carpenter?' (Mark 6.2,3)*

How *did* Jesus come by his qualities? We saw in *Book Two, Part 1* how Jesus spent time in prayer, engaging in the 'one-to-one ' relationship with God. Here we locate the 'deep well' from which Jesus drew the 'water of life' - the gospel. Communion with God, Maker of the universe and Lover of people, was the source of his power in word and deed. This spiritual 'meeting point' was Jesus' *'Holy of Holies'* (the term comes from the inmost place in the Temple of Jerusalem, where God and the high-priest meet). Prayer was the 'hub' of Jesus' religion, his life, from which the 'spokes' of all his concern and care for lonely or guilty people radiated. His mission to society in villages, towns, cities and the wider world was rooted in prayer.

Thus, one absolutely vital purpose of the Church is to help each human being to build his or her 'holy of holies', each one's inner, spiritual 'meeting point' with God. The Church has to help persons to realise that attractive and 'holy' though a St. Peter's in Rome or a St. Paul's in London may be, or their beloved parish church or chapel, it is no substitute for a place and moment - at best each day - where and when I can believe in/realise God's presence, tell God about my concerns, and seek God's guidance for my life. This place can be anywhere that I can be alone and without distraction: in a room at home, a secluded corner in an office-block, a street in the quiet of early morning, by a lakeside or atop a heather-moor:

> *'God is spirit, and those who worship him must worship in spirit and in truth.' (John 4.24)*

BUT how do we start to pray? We made out the case in *Book One, Part 2* for the reality of the Personal God, and for God's ability to communicate with us. God, the Author of all intelligence, wisdom, goodness and love wants to share all this with us who 'listen'.

The first step, then, is to believe in/realise that God is present, and is 'speaking' to us. The word 'speaking' is definitely a figure of speech. God communicates silently, just as we think silently and care silently - yet, really and truly. (The notion of our 'hearing voices' is misguided.) We may at the same time actually speak to God in audible words, because these can help us to form and develop our desires and understanding. I may for example begin my prayer with the words, *'Loving God, good morning.'*, or my search for guidance by saying, *'Please show me what is right.'* Yet essentially our prayer-speech is silent, in our soul.

And how can the Church bring people into this 'holy of holies'? Could not the whole Church 'take a good dose' of Quaker silence? A Meeting of the Society of Friends provides the place and time (about an hour) for persons to meet God with a minimum of distraction. Whilst in the hour members do speak or pray aloud, the greater part of the time is quiet - for 'conversation with

God'. Could not the whole Church gradually introduce once each month a silent Sunday Service?

Alternatively Church Members could mutually agree to keep a regular time for private prayer, or could met at frequent intervals to share silence together on any day. Silent prayer can also be aided by reading books by others who have 'conversed' with God. (A list is found in the *'Appendix')*

However, having advocated 'silent worship', such does need the supplement of audible words in the full growth of a Christian. Hymns, spoken prayers - free or 'set' - the reading and interpretation of the Bible, and preaching can all bring people into God's presence, and help us to understand God's character and purpose.

THE CHURCH - GOD'S LEISURE CENTRE

> *'IN GOD'S presence is the fullness of joy, at his right hand are pleasures for evermore.' (Psalm 16.11)*

Football team of Garstang Road Congregational Church, Preston

We saw in *Book Two, Part 1* how Jesus helped people to *relax* in God's presence, and encouraged them to take time-off from their mission to be refreshed. The Church today should also be such a community. For too long in its history the Church has been over-solemn, hyper-serious, a folk too much beating their breasts for guilt, or unyieldingly stiff with superior respectability: a society unable to enjoy life or 'let its hair down'. It has been seen from the outside as a 'kill-joy' people. Is this not one of the reasons why so many people have been - and still are - put off the Church?

A local Churches Together held a mission in the 1990s. Among many activities a Barn Dance was arranged. This was well-attended by Church members and their guests, and thc event began well with a light heart and some lively dancing. Then the guest evangelist was invited to give a 'message', and the rest of the evening was taken up by his lengthy preaching - and the dancing, jollity and camaraderie were drowned, as though they had no importance. (But now it's *confession time.* The author must hold up his hand and admit that once he used too long a time at a Church Christmas social speaking about the issue of justice. That was not well received!)

Conversely, the congregation where I was brought up - Sefton Road Congregational Church, Morecambe - understood the pattern of life voiced in the *Book of Ecclesiastes 3.1:*

> *'For everything its season,*
> *and for every activity under heaven its time.'*

Alongside the well-attended and ordered Services and dedicated Sunday School the congregation knew how to relax fully, as they held Saturday-night dances, hilarious concerts (there I learned the lyrics of *'Yes! we have no bananas'*, and *'Down Mexico way'!)*, as well as outings and games in the countryside.

The apostle, Paul, in his letter to the *Galatians 5.22* listed the gifts of God's Spirit; the first is *'love'*, and the second is *'joy'!*

When I was a minister in Oldham, Lancashire, in a sermon I drew - with a 'heavy brush' - a picture of sin. After the Service Bill Deaville, a Church Member and park-keeper, husband and father of three boys, possessing a rare combination of firm responsibility and puckish humour, came into the vestry. I have never forgotten his words to me:

'You know, Christianity is a happy thing!'

The Church must make sure to live as a community, a 'centre', providing both *LOVE* and *JOY!*

THE CHURCH - INTO ALL THE WORLD

'SPREADING EVERYWHERE' - the butter-retailer caught the customer's eye with this phrase, and the same phrase captures the mission of the Church and its good news.

Every true believer knows that as the human race is responsible for its own procreation, so he or she is charged and empowered by God to hand on the faith to other people. So, the Hebrew prophets felt the inner compulsion to share the truth God revealed to them. Amos the herdsman professed that God *'took me as I followed the flock... and said to me, "Go and prophesy to my people Israel".'* (*Amos 7.15*). Jeremiah felt constrained by God: *'Go to whatever people I send you.'* (*Jeremiah 1*).

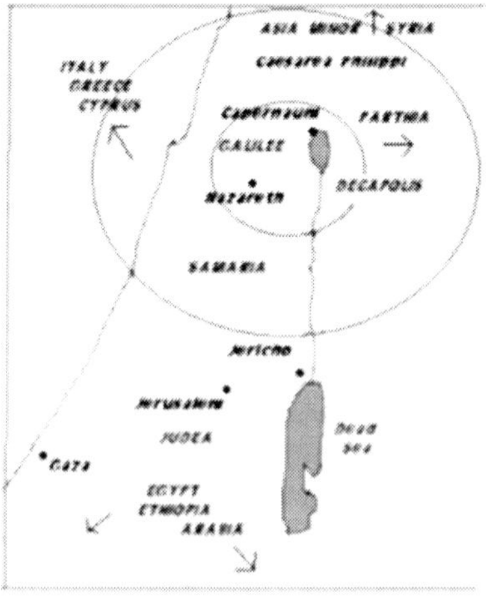

Jesus also, as we saw in *Book Two,* led his disciples to become *'fishers of men'*, apostles/messengers to their fellows: *'to proclaim my message... through the whole of Galilee.'* (*Mark 1.38-9*).

The 'mechanics' of mission then are basically one person meeting another to share faith, understanding and spiritual power; each believer steps out to meet another human being, wherever they are and in whatever circumstances they may be. The spread of Christianity around the world over almost two millennia has followed this pattern of Jesus and his first apostles, who journeyed to meet all sorts of folk: tax-collectors; a Roman centurion; rich people and beggars; men, women and children - without distinction - just human beings!

The mission spread ever wider as our map shows.

The following centuries saw Christians spreading like a fan ever further out ***into all the world,*** and now we just 'dip our toe into the sea' of this expanding Church.

AIDAN, an Irish monk, for instance, entered Northumbria in the 7th century, journeying mostly on foot to share his time and his faith with poor country folk as well as thanes and kings in their castles. English boys whom he educated and trained to be missionaries spread the gospel still further in their country, the brothers, Chad and Cedd, among them.

FRANCIS OF ASSISI in the 13th century dedicated his life to preaching and teaching among poor people. He, like Aidan, attracted many others to the mission, which grew into the Order of St. Francis, renowned for its preaching and outreach.

JOHN WESLEY in the 18th century employed the same means of person to person meeting.

He conveyed the 'warmth' of his faith to thousands of folk over large tracts of the British Isles as well as parts of North America, considering *'the world as my parish'.* He organised his colleagues into 'societies' in each place where his mission had reached.

JAMES CHALMERS, the 19th century Scottish missionary, was a pioneer of the Church in New Guinea. Once, warned about the bad physical conditions of an area of the big island, his response was: *'Are there men there?'* Meeting and caring for people was the paramount concern of the Christian mission.

This author witnessed this 'golden thread' of *meeting* in his childhood and youth. JOHN HOWARD DAVIES saw service as an ambulance man on the 'Western Front' in France up to 1918 before training for the Christian ministry. He became Minister of Sefton Road Congregational Church, Morecambe in 1922. For the next 43 years he shared the gospel, making contact with children and young people like me in Sunday School -as a member of staff- and youth fellowship, and with adults through his membership of several societies in the town - as well as in his inspiring sermons. Numerous people knew him as a minister and friend, spreading the gospel everywhere in the district.

IT is important to see the common factors in these examples of the spread of the Church.

- The personal, individual call of God to *'go to my people'*, and the determined response to stick to the commission, and 'stick the neck out' as a pioneer of the gospel.

- The development of a 'team' of apostles, whether proceeding two-by-two or in larger numbers. As pieces of coal catch fire by touching each other, so the 'fires' of love and service in Jesus' 'teams' have been kindled. Thus each team-member's special gifts may be developed, and mutual spiritual learning and growth may be furnished.

Today's Church must maintain these factors in order to spread the gospel to all humankind. (See the PARISH TEAM later in this *Part*).

CHRISTIANITY AND OTHER FAITHS

BUT NOW before we move on from *'spreading the gospel'* ,we must deal with a very 21st CENTURY question

> *'DO you want to convert every human soul - every Hindu, Buddhist, Jew, Moslem, as well as Pagans, Humanists and Atheists - into becoming Christians?'*

THIS truly is a hard question in that to give a straight answer, *'Yes' or 'No',* would involve misunderstanding of what *being a Christian* means, not to mention offending the honestly-held beliefs of members of other faiths. It will be useful, then, to say what is meant by ***being a Christian***. It means:

- being in a living relationship with Jesus;
- accepting his teaching about God as the Creator of the universe and Lover, Saviour and King of all people
- caring for everyone we meet day by day.

Given that definition, the Christian missionary would live and teach in order to help others to believe and act as a Christian would.

Such an aim and activity could be called 'conversion', but it is not meant to imply that we are calling on anyone to deny their present faith or practice, and it certainly does not employ coercion either physical or psychological to make someone change their religion. Thus it is not 'conversion' in any of those senses.

Another consideration is this. Whenever we meet someone who holds a different faith from ourselves, we must leave aside any prejudice or assumption about their faith, but on the contrary be open to their words and deeds. Why is this? Because, to begin with, we need to realise that God can reveal his nature and message to any human being at all times. (Book *One, Part 2, pp. 21-22)*

Thus there is no 'final revelation' as some faiths, including some versions of Christianity, assert. Moreover, this author's deduction, from study of various faiths, is that we should be prepared to find in them *both* true and worthy *and* untrue and unworthy elements. Is this not to be expected, given that widespread faiths are evolved by many imperfect human beings?

But how do we assess what is true or false in any religion? The answer is that religious truth must pass *three tests*

- *THE TEST OF SCIENTIFIC TRUTH, that is words that agree with the observation of our senses;*
- *THE TEST OF REASON, that is, 'Does it make sense?'*
- *THE TEST OF MORALITY, that is, 'Are people respected and cared for?'*

IT is further important that the Christian missionary should ask, *'How did Jesus himself view his mission?'*

We laid guidelines to tackle this query in *Book One, Part 3,* and in *Book Two, Parts 1 & 2.* Our study of the New Testament gospels led us to believe that we have to sift out authentic words of Jesus from words of later followers. Thus, there are passages in the Gospel according to John which do not appear to be authentic, because they are inconsistent with what seem to be the earliest *sayings collections* of Jesus. These passages from John have Jesus claiming a monopoly of the truth and authority and belittling the faith of others - as follows:

> *'The Father loves the Son and has entrusted him with complete authority.*
> *Whoever puts his faith in the Son has eternal life.*
> *Whoever disobeys the Son will not see that life; God's wrath rests upon him.' (3.35-6)*
> *'It is (God's) will that all should pay the same honour to the Son as to the Father. To deny honour to the Son is to deny it to the Father who sent him. (5.23)*
> *'The sheep paid no heed to any who came before me, for they were all thieves and robbers.' (10.8)*
> *'I am the way, the truth, and the life; no one comes to the Father except by me.' (14.6)*

C. K. Barrett in his contribution in *'Peake's Commentary on the Bible', p.849,* writes:

> *'The evangelist does not tire of bringing out the decision between belief and unbelief in the Son (i.e. Jesus) as the main point in the earthly ministry of Jesus, and thereby pressing it upon his readers also.'*

Such a stress on allegiance to Jesus as the chief message of Christianity has been the emphasis of much of the Church and its missionaries all through the centuries - and still today. But is it correct? Let us show why it is not!

A study of the three other Gospels shows us a quite different 'main point' of Jesus' ministry.

That Jesus was not self-centred or full of his own importance is seen when someone called him *'Good teacher'*, and he replied, *'Why do you call me good? No one is good except God alone.' (Mark 10.18)* No, Jesus was 'centred' on the needs of other people. He is eager to take the *'good news of God'* to as many people as possible.

> *'Let us move on', he says in Capernaum, 'to the neighbouring towns, so that I can proclaim my message there as well, for that is what I came out to do.' (Mark 1.38).*

The point of Jesus' mission according to *Luke's Gospel (9.2)* is to *'proclaim the kingdom of God and to heal the sick'.*

So far from seeking recognition for himself above all, he is, to quote the theologian, Dietrich Bonhoeffer, *'the man for others'!*

Now the further point should be made, that far from disdaining others' faith, Jesus showed appreciation. This he did in the instance of the Roman centurion, of whom he said, *'Truly I tell you: nowhere in Israel have I found such faith.' (Matthew 8.10)* Jesus also commends the insight of Hebrew prophets, quoting Isaiah's call for religion of the heart rather than ritual *(Mark 7.6),* and Hosea's urging mercy rather than sacrificial offerings (Matthew 9.13). And after all, was it not the historic Jewish commands that Jesus commended as the highest way of life - *'eternal life'*?

Even more than Jesus' words is the witness of his deeds of reverence for other people. Remember how he treated the 'heretic' Samaritans? When they refused him passage through their village, his disciples urged him to *'call down fire from heaven to consume them'.* Jesus refused and travelled another way. (Luke 9.51-6).

All this evidence provides a model for the attitude of Jesus' missionaries to people of various faiths. It wards off claims of Christian monopoly of truth, and any notion of converting others to Christianity by threats or 'arm-twisting'. Truth can 'stand upon its own feet' : it does not need the brute force or reputation of anyone to bolster it.

We may conclude then by outlining the constructive behaviour of the missionary to people of other faiths:

- realise that I have no monopoly of truth, but should never stop searching for it;
- meet as many people of others faiths as I can, listening to them and trying to understand, but also frankly questioning them about any feature of their faith that seems untrue
- or unworthy - yet, as Paul put it, 'in love';
- share Jesus' good news of God's love and mercy with all I meet, until all humankind is drawn together in respect and friendship.

THE SEMI-DETACHED CHURCH

JESUS was intensely concerned with God and the individual: the greatest command is *'love the Lord your God with all your heart..'* But Jesus continued: *'The second is this: "You must love your neighbour as yourself".'* (Mark 12.30-1). Human relations are also vital - as we saw in *Book Two, Part 2*, and Jesus' proclamation was *'the kingdom of God (society ruled by God) is upon you.'* So, we have applied Jesus' social ministry to general morality, family life, society-economy-nation and globally in *Book Three.* Here we just wish to look at the way in which the Church can contribute to the progress of the kingdom *of God* in human society.

THE CHURCH, the Christian assembly, is, like every community or phenomenon in the universe. It is within God's one creation. 'Sacred' and 'secular' are meaningless. At the same time the Church is like a SEMI-DETACHED HOUSE, which is on one side open to the wider scene, and on the other attached to another building just like itself. So, the Church is on one side open to the great God, and on the other open to people like the people in Church. The Church, then, must relate to God *and* to people. This dual stance presents the Church with some difficulty, which must yet be faced.

Here it is fitting to look at the Church as a 'PARISH'. The word 'parish' derives from the Greek, *'paroikia'* = 'district'. Simply, the Church takes responsibility for the people who live in a district/parish. The parish-principle is found in ancient Israel: the nation of Israel is deemed to be God's people and responsibility; each tribe of the nation has its own district; every soul is a member of the tribe and the nation, and is within God's, the king's and the chief's care.

Israel is one source of the parish system. Another is found in pre-Christian society, where landowners provided facilities for worship, and a priest, for their tenants. The Christian Church adapted and elaborated the parish system, yet leaving the principle of caring for every inhabitant in the parish intact. However, the concept of the parish came under criticism during the Reformation especially by the Separatists/Congregationalists. Robert Browne wrote in 1582:

> *'the kingdom of God was not to be begun by whole parishes (every inhabitant), but rather of the worthiest, were they never so few.' ('A Treatise of reformation without tarrying for any...')*

Browne called for 'gathered Churches' of the 'worthiest', independent of the state, and the 'established' Church.

We may commend the merits of the 'gathered Church':

> *Church Members' personal belief, freedom of thought and responsibility for the Church's life and mission; the service of Elders and government by Church Meeting.*

However, these 'separated' Churches in practice jettisoned the parish principle with its responsible care for every soul in its area. 'Separatist' Churches tended to become detached from 'the public' as a whole, and their needs.

Yet again, we return to the difficulty of the semi-detached position of the Church, particularly with its 'parish principle', and how it interprets its relation to God as well as to 'the public'.

As on the one side the Church relates to God, it must beware of presumption. It must, through prayer and thought, seek God's truth before speaking out for God. Did the Dutch Reformed Church in South Africa do this before it declared that non-white people were inferior beings in God's sight, and could be treated as such?

As on the other side the Church relates to fellow citizens, it should take the same care to ensure that it distances itself from popular prejudices and mores. Did the 'German Christians' do that before acquiescing to the Nazi's policy of persecution of the Jews?

The proper relation of the Church to God's kingdom and to the state is expressed in the United Reformed Church's 'Statement of Faith' (Article 8):

> *'The Lord Jesus Christ, the only ruler and head of the Church,*
> *has herein appointed a government distinct from civil government and*
> *in things spiritual not subordinate thereto, and that civil authorities,*
> *being always subject to the rule of God, ought to respect the rights of*
> *conscience and religious belief and to serve God's will of justice and*
> *peace for all humankind.'*

The Church, in summary, must really be *semi-detached*. It must seek God's will in due humility and insight, and act upon it with determination. It must also look on society and the state both with compassion and constructive criticism, and serve them with the same resolve as it serves God.

WHO'S IN CHARGE OF THE CHURCH?

THE nearest this author has come to the 'corridors of power' of the Church was at the lunch table in the residence of Alexis, Patriarch of Moscow and All Russia. With the opulence of gold cutlery on the table, the after-lunch conversation turned to the question of authority in the Church. Conflicting candidates for the primacy (top job) were the Pope of Rome and various Orthodox Patriarchs. I 'put in my two ha'porth', affirming that Jesus is the Head of the Church! 'Yes, that is the ideal', agreed a 'high-placed' Orthodox priest, but, he went on, we must face the practicalities of the present hierarchy.

This essay maintains the view that there is an authority in the Church transcending all Patriarchs, Popes, Moderators or Presidents. After all, Jesus proclaimed the kingdom/kingship of God, and proceeded, when his disciples disputed about who was the greatest among them, to warn against seeking precedence and privilege, and turned these 'on their head': the greatest is the servant - the very opposite of privilege!

At the same time Jesus delegated responsibility for the mission of the Church to others, because, if the life of the Church is to be active and developing, someone - one person or more - has to make decisions and turn resolution into action. Who is in charge?

Some in the Church believe the answer to be clear - as given in the *Gospel according to Matthew' (16.18)*: *(Jesus says) "you are Peter, the Rock; and on this rock I will build my Church."* However, detailed study of the New Testament raises serious objections to Peter as the 'primate'.

- The parallel passages of the incident in Mark's Gospel (8.27-33) and Luke's Gospel (9.18-22) do not have this delegation of status to Peter.
- James, Jesus' brother, appears to be leader in the 'mother' Church in Jerusalem. (Acts 15).
- Paul was in no way deferential to Peter, and publicly criticised him. (Galatians 2.11-14).
- There is much evidence of a power-struggle in the early Church between the followers of Peter and those of Paul. (See 'A Tale of Two Missions' by Michael Goulder).

Peter, then, was not in charge of the Church early on. Therefore there is no status to hand down to 'successors'!

AN enlightening discussion on this whole topic was taken up by Michael Taylor, at the time Principal of the Northern Baptist College, Manchester, at an ecumenical conference held in Liverpool in the 1970s. He raised several pertinent questions. Two of these were: Is one order or rule *in* the Church given *to* the Church? Or are there several alternatives? As illustrated above the second is the right answer. Decisions seem to be made by various individuals and groups in the Church described in the New Testament.

- Prophets and teachers, such as Manaen, ordain Barnabas and Paul to their mission. (Acts 13.1-3).
- Apostles and elders/presbyters, with agreement from the whole Church in Jerusalem, choose envoys to Gentile Christians. (Acts 15.22-3).
- Bishops are described as 'leaders' in 'The First Letter to Timothy' (3.1-7).
- Elders are equated with bishops in 'The Letter to Titus (1.5-9).

It seems then that we must ask the question one more time; *Who is in charge of the Church? Who is 'in authority'?*

Michael Taylor helpfully suggests that there are three types of AUTHORITY: *ABSOLUTE; RULING; INTRINSIC*

ABSOLUTE AUTHORITY claims always to know what is true; but even Jesus did not make such a claim. Is the claim really one person's desire to maintain power and privilege?

RULING AUTHORITY derives from an agreement between rulers and subjects, so that an organisation as numerous and widespread as the Church, world-wide or national or as a large local congregation, can agree to delegate decisions, with accepted conditions, either to individuals or groups/committees. This is a sensible, workable *authority*, preserving personal dignity.

INTRINSIC AUTHORITY belongs to the individual Christian.

So, a trained doctor decides treatment for a patient based not on hearsay or book-knowledge only but on his own thought and experience: that is *intrinsic authority*. Thus, intrinsic authority in the Church recognises the thought and experience of each Christian, when they gather to decide Church affairs together.

It seems to this author that the fitting *authority* of the Church is the combination of *ruling* and *intrinsic* forms. This is found in the *United Reformed Church*, whose *Basis* was agreed by the whole Membership at its foundation in 1972. Decisions are delegated to various individuals and groups within certain geographical areas: Assembly in the UK; provincial Synods; District Councils; local congregations, ruled by Church Meeting (comprising every Church Member), advised by elected Elders Meeting to whom certain responsibilities are delegated. Each area 'council' consults with the others when appropriate with a process of appeal to wider bodies when no agreement is achieved. Additionally, intrinsic authority is encouraged as the rights of personal conviction are upheld.

Here we have a Church, seeking God's guidance for its life and mission, well capable of making far-reaching decisions, as at the same time each Member is urged to take initiative on his or her own or in agreement with others.

A RENEWED CHURCH FOR A NEW MILLENNIUM

IF, Dear Reader, you have persevered with these writings thus far (excuse the Irishism!), you may well have adjudged that the author's view of what 'makes sense of life' is unorthodox or novel or unfashionable. Whereas loud voices in the 'mainstream' or 'free' or 'renewal' Churches are calling for a return to orthodoxy or even to 'that old-time religion' that was 'good enough' for our fathers and mothers, the 'voice' of this work has spoken up for modern science and fresh theology. We urge honest, constructive criticism of the Bible and the application of reasoned, moral principles to family life and to social, economic, political and global issues. Such a view of Christian faith and human life calls for a different kind of 'renewal' of the Church from the orthodox one.

The full description of this *renewal*, as the author sees it, would demand a whole volume in itself. Here we confine ourselves to a brief outline.

(The following paragraphs/sections are not necessarily in order of priority. Each topic is important and makes a contribution to the total renewal of the Church's life and mission.)

A CHURCH OPEN TO THE UNIVERSE AND ITS CREATOR

The Church must stimulate people to look at and comprehend the universe both in its grandeur and its fine detail, and to discover the 'hand of God' therein. Learning about God through nature has been decried by sections of the Church forgetting that prophets and psalmists - and Jesus - learned so much in the 'school of nature'!

SEEKERS AFTER TRUTH

The Church must encourage people to think for themselves, and to understand the ways of straight-thinking (or logic), such as the avoidance of generalisation (see instance above) and false assumption. How much do half-truths and shoddy thinking lead to misunderstanding, prejudice and strife! Back in the 17th century Roger Williams, a nonconformist Minister, published a book, 'concerning the tolerating of all sorts of religion'. Church authorities burned it! Williams reacted: 'I have little hope till those flames are over that this discourse against... persecution for cause of conscience will be acceptable, I say, not amongst the wolves and lions, but even amongst the sheep of Christ themselves.' How much the Church's 'ministry of the Word' and of 'reconciliation' demands the eager search for the truth still on our 21st century!

CRITICISM & INTERPRETATION OF THE BIBLE

Church Members must be exposed to the criticism and interpretation of the Bible of our modern times, which have helped to separate vital from unimportant strands of the Bible. We need to sift out the 'word of God' from the notions of men in the Scriptures.

FINDING AND LIVING THE CORE OF THE GOSPEL

The Church should seek and study the core of the Gospel, which is? *'The white-heat of the love of God.'* Then, that 'heat' should be reflected in passionate preaching, teaching and living. A revised Bible is needed. Whilst the present Bible should be kept intact as a *source* of religious knowledge, wisdom and revelation, the Church should patiently extract the *core* of the gospel, and supplement this with a summary of the findings of science and the annals of inspiring biography. (What an absorbing and challenging project for a team of Christian scholars!) This new 'Bible' should be produced as a text-book for people of all ages.

RESPONSIBILITY TO HUMAN SOCIETY

The Church must stress God's call to care for the life and troubles of society.

The *'social gospel'* must no longer be disparaged as an inferior, watered-down version of the 'true gospel' - as in this news-item:

> *CARDINAL GIACOMO BIFFI, Archbishop of Bologna, allegedly a leading contender to succeed Pope John Paul II, has recently derided philanthropy, concern for human and animal rights and the environment, vegetarianism, pacifism, and ecumenical dialogue between the Roman Catholic Church and other Christian denominations including the Anglican and Orthodox Church. Such social and unifying relations, suggests Cardinal Biffi, are the hidden 'agenda' of the Antichrist!*
> *Source: THE TIMES 7.3.2000*

Should the Churches of the 3rd Millennium be guided by persons with the views of Cardinal Biffi, they will decline further into irrelevance and uselessness. Why? Because it is the imbalance between the Church's time spent in worship compared with time given to society's need for harmony and justice that has seen large Christian communities live amid strife. Look at the evidence: persecution of coloured people in the USA; apartheid in South Africa; mutual slaughter of Moslems and Christians in Nigeria, Indonesia, Bosnia and Kosovo; Catholic and Protestant strife in Northern Ireland.

How much the Church needs to heed afresh the urging of Jesus:

> *'If you are presenting your gift at the altar and suddenly*
> *remember that your brother has a grievance against you,*
> *leave your gift where it is before the altar.*
> *First go and make your peace with your brother;*
> *then come back and offer your gift.' (Matthew 5.23-4).*

The Church must spend as much time among society as it spends at the altar, and must educate its folk in social/moral principles - love to neighbour and to 'enemy' - and apply them to family life, economics, politics and world-wide affairs.

'SHOUTING IT FROM THE HOUSETOPS'

Just as a shopkeeper can only attract the public to buy his wares by displaying them in his shop window, so the Church should ask for God's Spirit to give it boldness to 'broadcast' its Gospel: to go out from its walls into the 'open air', using every media - radio and TV, newspaper and magazine, pamphlet and poster, music and drama, video and internet - to tell folk about God's love.

THE PARISH TEAM

It is apparent that Jesus knew the value of *organisation*. The disciples were sent out on their mission 'two-by-two' and reported back after their journeys. Similar order is found in the Church described in the New Testament letters such as that to the *Ephesians (4.11-2)*:

> *'And it is Christ who has given some to be apostles,*
> *to equip God's people for work in his service,*
> *for the building up of the body of Christ.'*

We may adapt this team-pattern to the understanding of the Church's life and mission set out in this *Part*. So, if the Church is to be really effective in its varied mission - to love, to care, to pray, to relax and to evangelise, then this will best be achieved through a *team* of persons, in each place, whether a local congregation or a town or district, competent and zealous in each feature of the total mission. Something like this

TEAM-LEADER/MINISTER/PASTOR
WORSHIP LEADER SCHOLAR/TEACHER
STEWARD OF SOCIAL RESPONSIBILITY
EVANGELIST
RENEWAL & RECREATION LEADER

The members of this *parish team* could be stipendiary or not, and could well gather a number of Church Members to share his or her particular brief. The more people share responsibility the more effective both the Church and society as a whole will be. Our world has no greater need today than for *responsible, proactive, pioneering* men and women. The Church can produce them!

CHURCH MEMBERS EQUIPPED FOR MISSION

The Church needs to *train* its Members, preparing them with the tough qualities required. Which are?

- resolve to practise what is preached;
- ability to share and cooperate with others;
- willingness to pioneer fresh ways;
- strength to endure failure and resist resentment;
- preparedness for persecution.

NEW WINESKINS FOR A NEW ERA

THE CHURCH, as it moves into the 3rd Millennium, must in summary shed the encumbrance of every doctrine and practice that is incompatible with the MERCIFUL LOVE OF GOD, and the FACTS OF THE WORLD AROUND US that we can see and understand. Hence, the Church must publish the refined, clarified Gospel (Book *Two, Parts 1 & 2, and this Part)* and apply its principles to the life of humankind.

If the events of the 21st century move as rapidly as those of the 20th - such as the development of technology and speed-up of communications, together with the expansion of population from 2 billions in 1930 to 2.5 billions in 1950 to 5.3 billions in 1990 to (estimated) 8.5 billions in 2025 - then we shall witness heavier demands being made on human character and greater need for planning, sharing, conservation, tolerance and generosity.

This new era, therefore, will need a Church with mind wide open to the changing scene, and furnished with the self-same refined and clarified Gospel that is able to love and serve all the world's people with patience and charity. As Jesus put it: *'New wine goes into fresh skins.' (Mark 2.22).*

TWO CHRISTIAN SACRAMENTS

(i.e. Ceremonies witnessing to God's gracious gifts of personal and social salvation)

BAPTISM

THE term 'baptism' derives from a Greek word meaning *'to immerse in or wash in water'.* As a religious ritual the water's purpose was to purify body and soul.

So, for example, a Hebrew priest washed himself to become pure before offering sacrifice. (See *Exodus 40.12-15)* Similar rituals were performed in Greek and Roman ceremonies such as those for healing by the God, Asklepios.

As we come to the time of Jesus' ministry in Palestine we find ritual washing prominent in the Jewish sect of Essenes, and there is circumstantial evidence to believe that John (the Baptist) had belonged to this sect. John came to be convinced that he should go out to warn sinful people to change their ways -'repent'- before the imminent day of judgement. (See *Gospel according to Luke 3.1-17)* John called on his hearers to receive God's forgiveness, to be baptised as a sign of their change of heart, and to commit themselves to a life of good deeds.

Further evidence in the New Testament Gospels tells that Jesus joined John's movement and was baptised by him. Jesus later differed from John over the extent of God's mercy on sinners and on the meaning of the kingdom of God. (Book *Two, Part 2, pp. 56-57)* Yet, Jesus and his followers still believed deeply in God's forgiveness of sins for all people, and the ceremony of baptism persisted among the early Christians. (See *Letter to the Colossians 2.11-14)* The sacrament of baptism indeed remains as the ritual of entry to membership of most denominations of Christians to this day.

Unfortunately, even the most sacred features of any religion can cause controversy, and baptism is no exception. Should the rite be restricted to adults who can fully understand its meaning, or may infants who cannot possibly comprehend be baptised? Or again, can Quakers and Salvationists, who do not baptise, be regarded as members of the Christian Church?

The vital point is that any outward ceremony, however useful, is not as essential to the Christian soul as the inward, spiritual reality it is intended to aid. The rite may be dispensed with, but not the salvation of the soul!

So, if baptism is administered to an infant, it is required that adults -parents, godparents or Church Members- are responsible for helping the growing child to learn how to admit wrongdoing, experience God's mercy and change direction into right ways. The same sequence of transformation applies to any adult who embraces baptism.

BAPTISM, in summary, implies

CONVERSION - CONFESSION, ACCEPTANCE OF GOD'S MERCY and RECEPTION OF GOD'S SPIRIT OF GOODNESS BY WHOEVER RECEIVES IT.

HOLY COMMUNION

IT is no simple matter to describe this ceremony, because it has several different yet related aspects.

Let's begin by understanding the word 'communion'. It translates the Greek word, *koinonia* = 'sharing'. The apostle, Paul, uses this word to describe how, as Jesus *'shared'* bread and wine at his last supper with his disciples, so Christians 'share' the broken body (symbolised by bread), and the shed blood of Jesus (symbolised by wine) in this rite of 'Holy Communion'. It is 'holy' because Jesus is crucified for conveying *God's* commitment -*'covenant'*- to rebellious people. Jesus, at the last supper, says that God's 'new covenant' is sealed by his blood. (See Paul's *'1st Letter to the Corinthians', Chapters 10.16-7 & 11.23-6)*

So here we find another aspect of 'holy communion'. It tells of God's 'covenant', a word with a long history among the Jews. When God inspired the Israelites to escape from slavery in Egypt he was 'covenanting' (committing) himself to the people. They in turn covenanted with God, promising to keep God's laws, and the covenant was sealed by shedding animals' blood (See *Exodus 24.3-8*). Later, when the people broke so many laws, God forgave them and renewed his covenant: made a 'new covenant'. (See *Jeremiah 31.31-4)*

The mercy of God is another aspect of 'Holy Communion', and is of course central to the mission of Jesus. The strength of God's covenant -commitment- to humankind is shown: God does not desert us even when we abandon his ways.

> *'It was while we were still helpless that... Christ died for the wicked... and that is God's proof of his love towards us.' (Romans 5.6,8).*

So, 'Holy Communion' involves God and people mutually committing and sharing with each other. It also involves people committing and sharing with one another - as the disciples share at the Lord's Supper. The Israelites promise to keep God's laws that include respect for human life, marriage, property and reputation. Still today, the most worthwhile activities of life require commitment - from the most local -marriage, parenthood- through employment, public service to international relations. One translation of 'covenant' in Latin is 'fedus'. Every 'federation' is a commitment of people to each other; whether in Britain or Europe or anywhere. All cooperative endeavours need *committed* people, people who keep their promises *'to the edge of doom'.*

EACH TIME CHRISTIANS SHARE BREAD AND WINE IN HOLY COMMUNION, *in summary,* THEY ACCEPT GOD'S UNENDING GOODNESS AND MERCY and THEY COMMIT THEMSELVES TO SERVE GOD AND ALL PEOPLE ON GOD'S EARTH.

Snapshots of the Church's Mission

Top left: Somewhere in France - since early centuries the Church has lived among the people. Top right: INTO ALL THE WORLD - bridghead into England; St. Augustine's Cross in Ebbsfleet, Kent. Bottom left: Stone in front of Temple Sowerby Chapel, Cumbria, on which John Wesley preached 'The World is my Parish'. Bottom right: Celtic Mission to England - remians of Lindisfarne Priory, base of Aidan's ministry to Anglo-Saxons.

INTO the industrial age - the Church goes to the people, St. Thomas CofE, Oldham, Lancs

"We have a Gospel to proclaim..."
'Tell me the story simply, as to a little child...'

Taking the Gospel to the 'man in the street' - Salvation Army in Whitley Bay (right) - the Church on the move in Failsworth (left).

In the age of the automobile - open-air Worship in Pitlochry.

CHRISTIANS UNITE IN THE WORLD-WIDE CHURCH: Taiwanese guests in Sudbury (left). Russsian Orthodox Priest meets Salvation Army officers in Friends Meeting House, Canterbury (right).

MAKING SENSE OF LIFE - BOOK FOUR

THE CHURCH AND THE FUTURE

Part Two

The 3rd Millennium: World's End -or - 'Carry on Living'?

Catastrophe

OR

Building...

AND

Enjoying life in God's World

CARRY me back to green, green pastures,
that's where I want to be..
I know that there's a land of promise
waiting for weary souls;
carry me back to green pastures,
down where the Jordan rolls.'
'Deep river; my heart is over Jordan..'
'Swing low, sweet chariot,
coming for to carry me home..'

THESE lines of the 'spirituals' of the Afro-American slaves of the early 19th century speak of a mixture of deep despair and soaring hope.

The slaves were trapped in often cruel and degrading servitude with no possibility of return to their native Africa nor hope of freedom in America. Despair was inevitable. Yet, the Judaeo-Christian religion they acquired told them of eventual liberation in a 'promised land', just as their spiritual ancestors, the Hebrew slaves, achieved when they crossed the River Jordan into Canaan thousands of years before. But, the 'promised land' of the spirituals was not here on earth: it was in heaven. Like Elijah, the prophet of ancient Israel, they longed to be taken away from this cruel world to heaven in a 'chariot of fire' *(Second Book of Kings 2.11)*. The slaves yearned for the end of their miserable life on earth and the beginning of a joyous life in heaven. The end of *this* world could not come soon enough!

THE MILLENNIUM SYNDROME

THE experience of the slaves and their reaction to it is the stuff of the *Millennium Syndrome.*

A dictionary tells us that a syndrome is 'a set of signs and symptoms that together indicate the presence of a disease or abnormal condition'. Precisely, belief in *'The Millennium'* consists of a complex set of notions that trigger a jaundiced view of God and the world, and lead to abnormal, sickly behaviour, as we shall show.

Strictly speaking, *'The Millennium'* is one divine, cosmic event as described in *'The Book of Revelation' (20.4):*

> *'They (the Christian martyrs) came to life again and reigned for a thousand years.'*

However, during the history of Christianity this event has accumulated around itself an extensive set of 'symptoms' based upon many other Biblical texts and other traditions and writings. This set of symptoms is the *'Millennium Syndrome'.*

One of the Biblical texts referred to above is important because it contains many typical 'symptoms'. It is attributed to Jesus (probably incorrectly), and is found in *'The Gospel according to Mark, Chapter 13.* We list the topics of this passage and give some parallel references, which build up the full picture and traditional doctrine of *'The Millennium'.*

- *The Persecution of Believers - 'You will be handed over to their courts... beaten in the synagogues... on my account' (v.9).(Compare Daniel 11.29-35; Psalms 73.2-14 & 79; Revelation 2.8-10)).*
- *An Era of Wars- 'When you hear of wars and rumours of wars, do not be alarmed. Such things are bound to happen; but the end is still to come.' (vv.7,8) (Compare Isaiah 13.1-6; Ezekiel 38; Zechariah 12.1-13.1; Joel 3.9-12; Revelation 16.13-6 (Armageddon).*
- *Divine Retribution through a series of Natural Disasters - 'For those days will bring distress such as there has never been before since the beginning of the world... the sun will be darkened... the stars will come falling from the sky, the celestial powers will be shaken.' (vv.19,24-5). (Compare Amos 5.18-20; Isaiah 13.9-16; 2 Peter 3.7,10-12).*
- *Divine Counter-Attack, Victory and Return of Christ - 'Then they will see the Son of Man coming in the clouds with great power and glory, and he will send out the angels and gather his chosen from the four winds, from the farthest bounds of earth to the farthest bounds of heaven.' (vv.26-7) (Compare Daniel 7.9-14; Amos 9.8-15; Joel 3.13-21; 1 Thessalonians 4.13-18; Revelation 21.1-8).*
- *The End-Time is Near, but Inexact - '... the end is near, at the very door. Truly I tell you: the present generation will live to see it all... Yet about that day or hour no one knows..' (vv.29,30,32). (Compare Daniel 12.5-13; 1 Thessalonians 5.1-11; 2 Peter 3. 1-10; Revelation 3.3; 16.15).*

Such is the *Millennium Syndrome*. It is a complex of beliefs, but it has one chief cause - *persecution* - typified in *Mark (13.9):*

> *'You will be handed over to the courts; you will be beaten in the synagogues...'*

Thus, the persecution of the followers of Jesus has much in common with the oppression of the slaves in 19th century America and with the continual hounding of the Jews both in the ancient and the modern world.

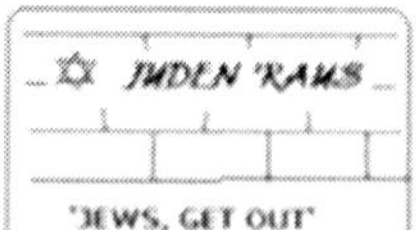

'JEWS, GET OUT'
THE HOUNDING OF THE JEWS IN NAZI GERMANY

So, we can summarise the common factors of the *Millennium Syndrome.*

- The victimisation of often innocent and religious people.
- The questioning by the victims; *'Why does Almighty God allow such*

injustice and pain?'

- The hope that 'soon' God will turn the tables on the oppressors and punish them , maybe through an appointed human or semi-divine Agent/Christ.

THE ILLUSION OF THE MILLENNIUM

WE may understand the strong logic of the Millennium doctrine; we may sympathise deeply with the yearning of persecuted people for *'an end to mourning, crying and pain' (Revelation 21.4)*, and for the coming of a Saviour-Christ.

Yet, we fail the truth and miss God's real purpose for humankind *here and now on Earth, and afterward in Heaven,* if we are afraid to face reality, and to demonstrate that the Millennium doctrine is an *ILLUSION,* acting as a 'red herring' across the path of real day-by-day living and a genuine faith in God.

Let us now justify this unorthodox but well-founded assertion.

DEFECTIVE MORAL THEOLOGY. One of the most powerful reasons for rejecting the *Millennium Syndrome* is its view of God's reaction to the persecution of the innocent and the violence of the oppressors. From the picture in *Isaiah 13.5* of God *'with the weapon of his wrath, laying the whole earth waste'* to the gory passages in the *Book of Revelation, Chapters 14 & 16,* telling of the fury of God against the wicked, we find the portrayal of a vengeful God. This is diametrically opposed to the merciful God known by the prophet, Hosea *(Hosea 11.2)*, and others in ancient Israel, and by Jesus, who, in the *First letter of Peter (2. 23)* is thus described: *'When he was abused he did not retaliate, when he suffered he uttered no threats, but delivered himself up to him who judges justly.'* We should also recall the findings of the 'Jesus Seminar' (Book *Two, Part 1, pp. 45-46)*: the teaching of God's wrath is not found in the Gospel-source, Q1. But in Q2 *'one hears the voice of a prophet pronouncing judgement on a recalcitrant world... and the sledge of apocalyptic threat'. (Burton L.Mack, 'The Lost Gospel' p.131)* The Millennium doctrine tells of a 'blitzkrieg' God, a God who has lost control of his temper, a God who uses the 'sledgehammer' of his almighty power to crack the nut of human offence. Such teaching has, to say the least, been no good example to the worst and cruellest tendencies of the most inadequate human nature.

A COUNSEL OF DESPAIR. The defective moral theology amounts also to a counsel of despair. We may agree with *Jeremiah (17.9): 'The heart (of man) is deceitful above any other thing.'* We are rightly appalled that humankind too often seems not to learn from its sins and follies. We lament with Elijah; *'It is enough; now, Lord, take away my life, for I am no better than my fathers before me.' (1 Kings 19.4)* And yet this despair was not the way of Jesus. His parable of The Sower tells of perseverance in the face of all setbacks. He counsels action for a better future 'against the tide' of human hatred and vengeance:

'Love your enemies... If anyone slaps you on the right cheek, turn and offer him the other also.' He refuses to 'bring down fire' on the Samaritans who bar his way to Jerusalem. However religious people may believe that demonic powers control the nations, Jesus proclaims that God is king here and now on earth; *'The kingdom of God is in your midst.' (Luke 11.21)*

Far from destroying imperfect folk, he heals the sick, 'casts out devils' from people, and brings repentance and salvation to those who are 'lost'.

Yet so many people have experienced violence from individuals and groups and attack from warrior-nations that they still are convinced by the foretelling of *'wars and rumours of wars... earthquakes and famines',* and have become resigned to such 'divinely-ordained' events. So, they believe that it is useless to act to prevent conflict or war. 'How can we work against what Jesus or God has foretold and ordered?' they ask.

We need to be honest and bold enough to reply, 'Jesus has foretold no such thing. You should not accept such prophecies. Wars are started by selfish people: not by God. The future is open: the choice of good or bad is yours. With God's help you can shape the world in the form of love, harmony, peace and joy!' This we shall see.

A SERIOUS MISUNDERSTANDING OF HISTORY - AND OF GOD. We have already noted that the passage in *Mark 13* about the world's end and the return of Christ is probably not a record of what Jesus said. One of the chief reasons for this note is that Jesus taught that the kingdom of God is present (Book *Two, Part 2, pp. 56-57*): we don't have to wait for it as *Mark* suggests. Furthermore, most of the predictions in *Mark 13* just did not happen: see especially *vv. 24-6, 29-31.*

A vital factor to be considered in this subject is the *reality* of the history of the world. However much insight our ancestors, alive in Biblical times, possessed about the scale of time and space, they, as far as we know, did not have the instruments and other tools of knowledge, such as space satellite-dishes in the field of astronomy, nor the tools of physics and archaeology that have been made available to scientists especially in the 20th century. Consequently we are now aware of an infinitely larger scale of time and space. *(Book One p. 18)* Biblical authors could envisage the stars falling from their fixture in the firmament-dome

several thousand miles above the flat earth. The reality now discovered is vastly different in terms of scale, and both astronomy and space-travel reveal the true position of the stars, many millions of miles away from Earth.

It is moreover stretching sense and credulity very far to believe that God, whose universe has existed for possibly 15 billion years, and has engaged God in the most ingenious, painstaking and artistic planning (Book *One, Part 1)* would destroy that creation. Still further, human life has inhabited this planet for millions of years, and the follies and sins of people have in all probability persisted throughout most of that time. We can conclude then that God is not of a nature to be exasperated, lose his temper and obliterate his creatures, but rather of a nature to be patient, always giving time for a change of heart. So history shows! There is, by the way, no evidence for a destructive world-wide flood, caused by God's wrath as told in *Genesis 6-8.*

'PIE-CRUST' PROMISES ARE NOT GOD'S STYLE

'THE end is near; at the very door.' (Mark 13.29) This Gospel-prediction is bolstered by the promise Jesus is believed to have given by the author of the Book of Revelation' (22.20): *'Yes, I am coming soon!'*

These prophesies have not been fulfilled. They probably were never made! And even if they had been made, is it not honest to say that it is wrong and irresponsible to promise an event to take place 'soon', and then keep people waiting for over 1900 years? To do this is to waste people's time - and God's. It is as wrong and cruel as keeping a convicted man on 'death-row' for years on end whilst legal wrangling proceeds. To make promises that this wicked world is soon going to end, and urge people to anticipate it, when that event is to be years, even centuries, ahead, is a cruel deception. That is not the style of God, who gives hunger, but who meets that need faithfully - and 'soon' - in the regular harvest!

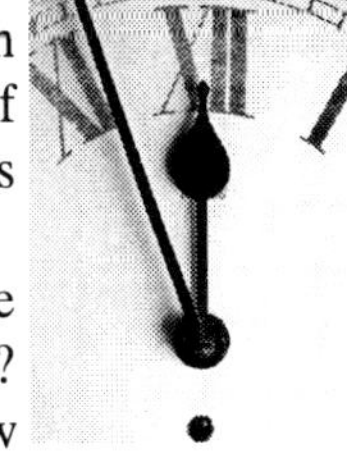

The illusory Millennium predictions also distract people from God's actual purposes for life on Earth. Expecting the imminent world's end has incited folk to act like employees in a factory, who watch the clock for the end-of-shift instead of getting on with the work they were engaged to carry out. This distraction has happened too often among believers.

How many small-scale instances - yet disturbing for those involved - of waiting for the return of Christ have occurred? A teenage schoolgirl in the 1970s persuaded some of her fellow pupils to stop preparing for important examinations, because such would be pointless in the Millennium which was about to begin!

Far worse incidents have been triggered over the centuries, as when in 999 AD. a spate of comets and natural disasters prompted outbreaks of mass panic, chaos and wild behaviour.

Mesmerised by the contemplation of Bible-texts, pious individuals have confidently predicted the end-time. Mother Shipton in the 15th century declared that that the end-time would be in 1991. Archbishop Ussher in 1650 calculated the last days for 1996, that is 6000 years after the 'days of creation' in 4004 BC. C.T. Russell, founder of the Jehovah's Witnesses, predicted the end to be in 1914. The Witnesses later revised the date to sometime before 1984! The sad illusion persists. Here is an instance

> *KANUNGU, UGANDA, 17 March 2000*
> *OVER 300 followers of Joseph Kibwetere, who had predicted that the world would come to an end on 31 December 1999, and believed that the Virgin Mary had promised to carry them to Heaven, were burned to death in a mass killing in their place of worship.*

What a tragic waste of human life! It leads this author to believe that, should a *Revised Bible* be compiled (see p.4-22), no passages about a violent end to the world should have any place in it!

WE may conclude that the doctrine of the *Millennium* is an ILLUSION. We may call it 'HOLY CLOCK-WATCHING' - a waste of the time of God and humankind! God, you and I, rather, may best enact the virtues of diligence and patience.

'PATIENCE IS A VIRTUE'. Absolutely. God knows that, to develop patience, we need *time* on Earth. So, for example the modern microphone developed from the invention of Bell in 1876. Bell himself was patiently prepared for his labours in Edinburgh and London Universities, and went on to invent the gramophone

Is not the reality that, we may so put it, God has signed us on in a 'factory', whose address is 'EARTH'? Our work, our life, is here for as long as the body God has given to us can last. Here we 'put our hand to the plough', and should not be distracted, 'looking back', wishing we weren't here!

GOD put us here on his good Earth to learn how to 'keep our eye on the ball' - to be reliable, diligent, happy, and above all to love each other..

CARRY ON LIVING? - YES!

MANY thousands of human beings alive today base their activity, most reasonably, in the tacit belief that as God has sustained the Earth for millions of years, this planet will carry on for years, decades, centuries into the future. Who are these people? They are house and bridge-builders, medical scientists, forestry planners, research and develop-

ment leaders. Such folk plan not only for their own careers, but for the benefit of generations to come. They are truly people 'made in God's image', the great, Patient Planner. (Book *One, Part 2)*. They are a living rebuke to the notion of an imminent end of this world, and a testimony to this faith: that the purpose of God is to maintain this planet into the 3rd millennium and the 4th - and beyond!

What reasons do we give for the endurance of God's plan for Earth?

2000 YEARS OF EVIDENCE

SOME of the early Christians believed, as we have seen, that God was about to bring the Earth and its inhabitants to a catastrophic end. According to that belief there should be no 21st century AD.: not even a complete 2nd century! *'Man proposes; God disposes.'!*

Just think of it! Had God destroyed the Earth in, say, 100 AD., millions of people would have been denied the joy of thrilling, sublime MUSIC: no 'Trumpet Voluntary' by Jeremiah Clarke, no 'Jesu, Joy of Man's Desiring' by J. S. Bach, none of Mozart's 'Eine Kleine Nachtmusik', Beethoven's 'Choral Symphony', Percy Grainger's 'Shepherd's Hay'; no operettas of Gilbert & Sullivan or Edward German.

We should never have been enthralled by the God-given VOICES of Caruso or Pavarotti, Isobel Baillie or Kathleen Ferrier, Paul Robeson or Frank Sinatra.

No masterpiece PAINTINGS would exist from the hands of Michaelangelo or Rubens, Gainsborough or Constable, Renoir or Picasso.

If God had destroyed the Earth in 100 AD., we could not have laughed at the COMEDY of Charlie Chaplin, Laurel & Hardy, or George Formby.

Certainly in the last 2000 years there has been so much suffering and wickedness: the persecutions of Nero and Caligula, the cruel invasions of Attila the Hun, William the Conqueror - and the rest!

The Black Death of the 14th century and the 17th century Great Fire of London; epidemics of cholera, diphtheria and malaria, the scourges of cancer and arthritis have brought misery to thousands - as have the continual incidences of barbarism: the Jewish 'holocaust', the 'killing- fields' of Cambodia, the genocides of Rwanda and Burundi. None of this would have occurred.

And yet, neither would the tender care day after day of innumerable doctors and nurses, faithful husbands and wives, sons and daughters, tending loved-ones in their need.

John Howard would never have pioneered more compassionate treatment of prisoners. Florence Nightingale would never have healed the woeful soldiers of the Crimean War. Louis Pasteur would not have introduced vaccination against many diseases. There would have been no Louis Braille to invent a form of 'writing' that blind people could 'read'.

The strange but true fact is that the blackness of adversity shows up the light of human courage and devotion. -

VENELA, MOZAMBIQUE, 5 March 2000

A helicopter drops relief-food to a crowd of hungry flood-refugees. Some of the children have lost their parents. One child is called Jorge, 5 years old. He is crying with hunger pains and chewing his shirt. Suddenly, a foil-wrapped package drops at his feet and Jorge starts to peel open the precious gift. His two big brothers and another boy make no attempt to grab the high-energy biscuit. Jorge continues to reveal the wafer with his fingers - and then breaks it into separate pieces and hands them around among the other children, before eating the last segment himself.

Such an act of extraordinary caring highlights the attitude and words of John Bosco, who reclaimed, housed and educated boys from the slums of Turin in the 19th century:

'We live in troublous times and it seems madness to found a new religious congregation at the very moment that the world and hell together are doing all in their power to wipe out those that already exist. But be not afraid. It is not probabilities but certainties that I am telling you. God is blessing our endeavours and desires them to continue.'
(J.H.Adels, 'The Wisdom of the Saints', p.57)

SO, for almost 2000 years since the world's end was said in the New Testament to be coming *'soon'*, God has continued his eternal plan - God has given humankind life on Earth, freedom to seek the truth, and grace to choose the better over the worse. Many over the centuries have strayed and reaped tragedy and pain, yet God has not withdrawn his love and providence.

'While the earth remains, seed-time and harvest shall not cease.'

Thus, all who have known God's care over two millennia urge us in chorus:

'Carry on living on the Earth, we did - by the grace of God!'

PROGNOSIS FOR PLANET EARTH -
'SHOULD DO WELL FOR AGES'

YOU can never be sure of course. A builder inspected the chimney-stack at the Manse in Oldham in the 1960s. His verdict: 'Nothing to worry about: it should be ' all right for some time.' A month later a gale-force December wind blew. The loud bang of bricks falling on the kitchen-roof caused me to turn a pan into a helmet. The chimney-stack had to be rebuilt!

So, whilst the Earth has existed for over 4000 million years, it has had its catastrophes. Some calamity wiped out the dinosaurs. Ice ages have disrupted humankind's habitation of the planet. A comet could some day collide with the Earth, and cause immense damage. Yet, for all that, the extended endurance of the Earth so far, and the estimate that the Sun with its nuclear fusion has enough hydrogen available to remain active as Earth's source of heat and light for at least another 5000 million years supports our trust that God *is* saying to us:

'CARRY ON LIVING!'
BUT WHAT ABOUT A NUCLEAR ARMAGEDDON?

New York - 9/11

THE first atomic bomb fell on Hiroshima on 6 August 1945 and cremated almost 100,000 people. That event signalled the start of the nuclear arms-race, producing devices far more powerful than the A-bomb. The human race is now capable of its own suicide, indeed of destroying all human life many times over. However, should a war waged with nuclear weapons ever take place, this would not have the same cause as the 'battle of Armageddon', mentioned in the *Book of Revelation (16.16)*. There the cause is said to be the evil will of supernatural beings, *'demonic spirits' (16.14)*. Such spirits are the fantasies of traditional imagination.

No, nuclear war would have very human causes: fear or thirst for power or war-fever, or selfishness or religious fanaticism.

> *'Fundamentalist powers, each armed with nuclear warheads and a Messiah, should effectively shorten human history.' (Kenneth Robinson, 'The Way and the Wilderness, p.89)*

> *Nuclear war with its horrors*
> *and terrorist atrocities*
> *would not be down to the God of mercy,*
> *but to human folly.*

THE CHALLENGE OF THE NUCLEAR ERA

THE destructive potential of nuclear weapons presents a challenge to us all. This has been put by several wise people;

> *'We must learn how to live together, or we shall die together!'*

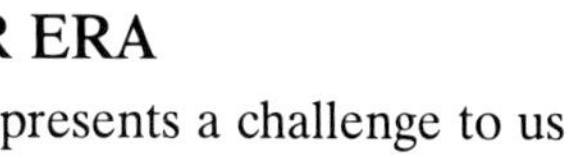

Learning how to live together is one of the chief reasons for God's creation (Book *One, Part 2, p. 27-*

28) God gives us freedom to choose right or wrong, love or hate. This eternal choice is now more vital than ever, and we have set out the way to peace in *Book Three, Part 4*. Only through living by moral principles can we look forward to 'doing well' in the 3rd millennium.

HOW SHOULD WE 'CARRY ON LIVING' IN THE THIRD MILLENNIUM?

AS we begin yet another millennium, we could be tempted to fall into the 'Ecclesiastes Mood'

> *'All things are wearisome... what has happened*
> *will happen again... there is nothing new under the sun.'*
> *(Book of Ecclesiastes 1.8,9)*

We have a modern expression: *'Been there; done that!'* Yet such thoughts *'miss the many-splendoured thing'* that life can *be.* Paul caught the better mood of anticipation:

> *'Things beyond our seeing... things beyond our imagining,*
> *all prepared by God for those who love him.'*
> *(1 Corinthians 2.9)*

Robert Browning also stated human hope, thus:

> *'Grow old along with me!*
> *The best is yet to be, the last of life, for which the first was made:*
> *Our times are in His hand who saith 'A whole I planned,*
> *Youth shows but half; trust God: see all, nor be afraid.'*

Moreover, we should always realise that here on Earth we live in God's presence every day, year, century, millennium. God's spirit is always encouraging people to grow in ability and achievement. Thus, we have recalled the fine people and deeds of the last two millennia. People of vision like Arthur Hugh Clough, who wrote:

> *"Say not the struggle naught availeth,*
> *The labour and the wounds are vain,*
> *The enemy faints not nor faileth,*
> *And as things have been they remain.*
> *If hopes were dupes, fears may be liars;*
> *It may be, in yon smoke concealed,*
> *Your comrades chase e'en now the fliers,*
> *And, but for you, possess the field.'*

What kind of people, then, will grace the Earth in the coming years; what deeds will they perform?

WE have tried all along to *MAKE SENSE OF LIFE.* The author's wish is that the best of life referred to here may be developed in our future. How then shall we live?

GOALS FOR A BETTER FUTURE

- Appreciate the stupendous universe
- Seek to know and commune with my Creator
- Grow in knowledge, reason and commitment
- Learn more about Jesus, so as to ' follow him more nearly day by day'
- Establish moral principles and live by them
- Cherish my family and renew my devotion to them
- Contribute to the well-being of my nation, Church and wider world

GOD has given us life's' journey to complete: a journey under endless skies, and surrounded by vast resources. We have received a body strong enough to travel the road day after day. And we do not walk alone. We share the journey, giving and receiving, with all humankind.

'RETURN TO SENDER'

'YOU, (O God) turn mortals back to dust, saying,
"Turn back you children of mortals".' (Psalm 90.3)
'Brief life is here our portion, brief sorrow, short-lived care;
the life that knows no ending, the tearless life is there.'

From the ancient psalmist to Bernard of Cluny, quoted above, poets tell the truth, that eventually all our human achievements on Earth turn to dust. It is an undeniable fact that the span of our earthly life and our stature are minute compared with the infinity of time and space. It all appears to be pointless, as an elderly Yorkshireman once said to me: *'When you're dead, you're done!'*

AND YET - THERE ARE POINTERS TO ETERNAL LIFE

William Wordsworth wrote:

'Our birth is but a sleep and a forgetting;
The Soul that rises with us, our life's Star,
Hath had elsewhere its setting, and cometh from afar;
Not in entire forgetfulness, and not in utter nakedness,
But trailing clouds of glory do we come from God who is our home:
Heaven lies about us in our infancy!'

POINTERS TO ETERNAL LIFE

I realise that life continues before I am
born and after I die
GOD HAS PUT ETERNITY INTO MY SOUL

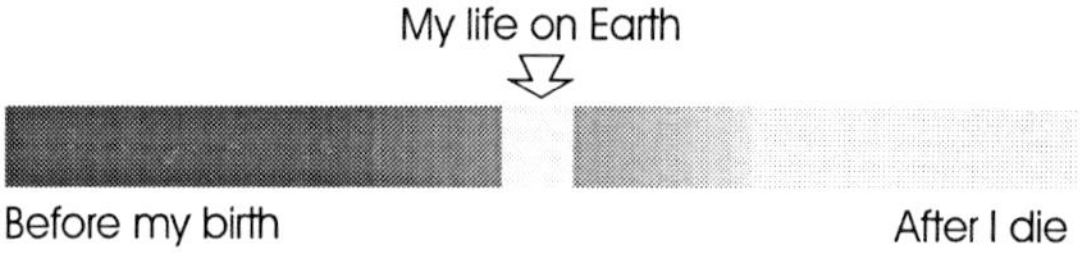

"'Tis the Divinity that stirs within us;
'Tis heaven itself that points out an hereafter,
And intimates eternity to man."
(Joseph Addison)

So, we affirm with Longfellow:
"Life is real! Life is earnest! And the grave is not its goal;
Dust thou art, to dust returneth, was not spoken of thy soul"

I experience in my life here today,
timeless, spiritual dimensions like
truth, courage and love.
I am cared for by the eternal God,
and Jesus is my ever-living friend.

Before Here & Now After

THE EVER-LIVING GOD

MY *body* will not see most of the 21st century! But I believe that my *soul* will 'journey on' with for God for ever. as *Job* put it:

'Without my flesh I shall see God.' (19.26)
My body will return to God's earth,
and my soul to my Maker in heaven.

WHAT WILL HEAVEN BE LIKE

I KNOW AS LITTLE about Heaven as I did about my future life on Earth on the day I was born, 24th September 1929! Yet, I anticipate!

And, the gist of what I anticipate is voiced in the message of the World Council of Churches Assembly in Evanston:

'We do not know what is coming to us;
but we do know who is coming.'

Heaven's 'geography and history' are beyond our ken, but we shall be meeting the same God in Heaven that we have met on Earth.

The God who has created a beautiful Earth will create a beautiful Heaven.

The God who has loved us, forgiven us and redeemed us HERE, will love, forgive and redeem us THERE!

SO, I just look forward to the continued adventure God has prepared for me - and for you, Dear Reader and Friend, and I conclude by commending to you the faith expressed in John Greenleaf Whittier's hymn, my Mother's favourite in her closing years on Earth. (Read the whole hymn in *'Congregational Praise', 407):*

'I know not what the future hath of marvel or surprise,
Assured alone that life and death God's mercy underlies.
I know not where God's islands lift their fronded palms in air;
I only know I cannot drift beyond God's love and care.'

****

Further Reading

BOOK ONE

Part 1

Paul Davies: 'The Mind of God' (Penguin)

Russell Stannard: 'The God Experiment'

Part 2

Ninian Smart: 'Dimensions of the Sacred' (Fontana)

Matthew Fox: 'Original Blessing' (Bear)

Tony Lane: 'Concise Book of Christian Thought (Lion)

Part 3

James Barr:'Fundamentalism' (SCM)

Georg Fohrer: 'History of Israelite Religion' (SPCK)

BOOK TWO

John Dominic Crossan: 'The Historical Jesus'and 'Jesus: A Revolutionary Biography' (Harper Collins)

Burton l. Mack: 'The Lost Gospel' (Element)

Edward Schillebeeckx: 'Jesus' (Fount)

E.P.Sanders; 'The Historical Figure of Jesus' (Fount)

Charlotte Allen: 'The Human Christ' (Lion)

N.T.Wright & Marcus Borg: 'The Meaning of Jesus' (SPCK)

BOOK THREE

Part 1

Jimmy Boyle, 'A Sense of Freedom (Pan)

Jostein Gaarder, 'Sophie's World (Phoenix)

Percy Dearmer, 'The Legend of Hell' (Out of Print)

Part 2

'The Wedding Service' (United Reformed Church)

Part 3

Will Hutton: 'The State We're In' (Vintage)

'Unemployment and the Future of Work' (Council of Churches for Britain & Ireland)

Part 4

'Charter of the United Nations'; and UN Universal Declaration of Human Rights' (UN Association)

BOOK FOUR

Part 1

Michael Goulder: 'A Tale of Two Missions' (SCM)

Philip Newell:, 'Listening for the Heartbeat of God' (SPCK)

David l.Edwards: 'English Christianity' (Fount)

'The Manual' (United Reformed Church) (Devotional Reading)

Steve Brown: 'Approaching God' (Summit)

George Appleton: 'Oxford Book of Prayer'

David Adam: 'The Edge of Glory' (Triangle)

Leslie Weatherhead: 'A Private House of Prayer' (Arthur James)

Mother Julian: 'Revelations of Divine Love (Penguin)

'Guidelines to the Bible' (Bible Reading Fellowship)

'Words for Today' (I.B.R.A.)

'Collins Gem Book of Prayers'

Part 2

Norman Cohn: 'The Pursuit of the Millennium' (Paladin)

Elizabeth Goudge: 'A Book of Faith' (Spire)

Biblical References

Index of People

Main Themes

Making Sense of Life - Malcolm Hill

Malcolm Hill tells of his life's journey guided by faith in the God of love and mercy. He sees the whole universe as the work of the Personal God, who brings all creatures into existence in a world overflowing with resources and opportunities. God also makes us free to choose our way of life. This freedom can result in well-being or disaster. Yet, however we use our liberty, God persists in his care for us. God is aware of our weakness, fears and wrongdoing, but always reacts with guidance and mercy.

The author gains inspiration for this faith especially in the Bible, which however he does not find to be an infallible guide. Rather, the Bible is like a river-bed from which we may extract truth like gold from amongst slag. He particularly values the critical investigation of the New Testament Gospels carried out by the 'Jesus Seminar', a group of American scholars. Their researches have revealed a historical Jesus, who proclaims God's persistent forgiveness of our wrongs, and encouragement to right-living.

Malcolm Hill proceeds from here to show how God's love and mercy aid us in our moral behaviour, whether within our soul or in our family life, our wider society, our economic and political relationships as a nation and worldwide. The survey of Christian faith and human life is rounded up by a blueprint for the Church's mission among humankind, and an assessment of the future of life on this planet - and beyond.

The work as a whole is intended as an *introduction* to a sensible faith and a constructive life in the contemporary world.

Can you make sense of life? Read on.